Endorsement

"Françoise Mastroianni gets it. She understands healing from sexual integrity issues is not about stopping destructive behaviors, instead it is about transformation of the heart, or as she puts it *becoming*. After spending years helping men manage their problematic sexual behaviors, and having been a betrayed partner, Françoise has captured the true essence of what recovery is all about. She walks the reader through the stages of recovery, ranging from the basics to what is needed to help the betrayed partner heal. She describes the attitudes that will lead to success as well as the potential pitfalls. A must-read for all who are about to embark on the journey of recovery and healing from sexual integrity issues."

Eddie Capparucci, Ph.D., LPC, CSAS
Author of *Going Deeper: How the Inner Child Impacts Your Sexual Addiction*
Abundant Life Counseling
Highlands, NC

BECOMING

A Guide to Recovery from Sexual Addiction While Helping Your Partner Trust Again

FRANÇOISE MASTROIANNI

Becoming: A Guide to Recovery from Sexual Addiction While Helping Your Partner Trust Again

Copyright © 2025 Françoise Mastroianni
Published by Market Refined Publishing
193 Cleo Circle
Ringgold GA 30736
marketrefinedmedia.com

All rights reserved. No part of this publication may be reproduced, distributed, or transmitted in any form or by any means, including photocopying, recording, or other electronic or mechanical methods, without the prior written permission of the publisher, except in the case of brief quotations embodied in critical reviews and certain other noncommercial uses permitted by copyright law.

Unless otherwise indicated, all Scripture quotations are taken from the Holy Bible, New Living Translation, copyright © 1996, 2004, 2015 by Tyndale House Foundation. Used by permission of Tyndale House Publishers, Carol Stream, Illinois 60188. All rights reserved.

Print ISBN: 979-8-9924512-6-9

Digital ISBN: 979-8-9924512-7-6

LCCN: 2025907750

Cover and Interior Design by Nelly Murariu, Pix Bee Design

Manuscript Edits by Ariel Curry of Ariel Curry Editorial and Market Refined Media & Publishing

Printed in the United States of America

First Edition: June 2025

Dedication

I dedicate this book to the love of my life, Dan.
I love you now more than ever.

Table of Contents

Note from the Author	vii
Introduction	ix
Chapter 1: Commitment to Rigorous Honesty	1
Chapter 2: Disclosure	19
Chapter 3: The Trauma Model	41
Chapter 4: Your Brain on Shame and Other Emotions	61
Chapter 5: Working a Twelve-Step Program	71
Chapter 6: Helping You Heal	85
Chapter 7: Wait with Expectation	107
Chapter 8: Be of a Sober Mind	117
Chapter 9: Radical Love and Transformation	125
Chapter 10: Peace and Prosperity	143
Conclusion	161
Acknowledgments	165
Recommended Resources	167
Organizations and Additional Resources	169
Endnotes	171
About the Author	177

Note from the Author

This book includes real life stories *used with permission,* drawn from my personal experience and the experience of several of my clients. To maintain the anonymity of others, in some instances I have changed client names, any identifying characteristics, and details of events.

Every story included is intended for educational purposes only and illustrates the heart and healing behind each individual's journey as they committed to recovery and engaged in the hard work of becoming who they are meant to be.

My wish for anyone who struggles with sexual integrity issues is that you hold on to the hope of recovery and begin to rebuild your life in healthy ways—both for you and your partner.

Introduction

> "You become. It takes a long time. That's why it doesn't happen often to people who break easily, have sharp edges, or must be carefully kept. Generally, by the time you are Real, most of your hair has been loved off, your eyes drop out, and you get loose in the joints, which is very shabby. But these things don't matter because once you are Real, you can't be ugly, except to those who don't understand."
>
> *The Velveteen Rabbit* by Margery Williams

This book is about sexual integrity issues and the recovery process from compulsive behaviors that stretch beyond a one-night stand or a single emotional or physical affair. I write to the man whose sexual behaviors and thoughts are out of control, negatively impacting his life financially, emotionally, physically, spiritually, and relationally, especially with his partner. I'm not writing from the place of some of the great writers and psychologists in my field, but rather as a licensed clinical professional counselor, pulling from my own personal experience and that of my clients. I've also received several certifications in the field of trauma and addiction. The clients I refer to have been in the trenches of sexual addiction and difficult times, but they have also experienced a change of heart and healing. Consider my writing as a letter that gives you hope and an understanding of yourself, your partner, and how this addiction impacts both of your lives. My hope for you is that you open your heart and mind to a recovery process to help you move through your trauma and addiction and help your partner in the aftermath of sexual addiction-induced trauma.

I am writing from my heart and hoping that you will receive this letter as though we were sitting across from one another. Consider Robert, whose heart has been shut down and ripped open from the indiscretions and losses of his sexual addiction. He began to heal and have hope, only to be torn up again. He is caught in a web of divorce and co-parenting, while still in love with his ex. They text at least twice a day, and she shares stories of the new love in her life. Robert has a hard time telling Missy how hard it is to hear her stories of the man she is about to marry; he feels needed and a part of her life, and he wants to stay connected to her in any way possible. He loves that she can confide in him. I intervene and encourage Robert to tell her the truth about his feelings for her—to set communication boundaries and to stay connected only through matters directly concerning their daughter. Giving redirections like that are so hard to say when I see Robert suffering. Recovery work is not linear; it's up and down and all over the place. As I come alongside and walk through the journey with Robert, I respect his choices and understand how difficult it is for him. I pray for him in our sessions and check in on him. I cannot be present with you in the same way I am with Robert, so instead, I write this for the hurting hearts that have similar stories.

Grab a cup of coffee and settle into a quiet place where you can focus your attention on what I would like to share with you.

This is a letter about *becoming*—becoming who you can be without *breaking easily*, becoming who and what you were meant to be and do *once you are real*. Becoming takes us to a level of maturity, knowledge, emotional intelligence, and spiritual wisdom. It is never without cost and unexpected consequences. This *becoming* happens over time; it's a process of growth and development of the true self. This work requires endurance, commitment, and a rigorous loyalty to the process as you start to put off the old, false self and put on the new, real self.

The shedding and elimination of behaviors, habits, and patterns that have destroyed and stripped you of the old self will also "cleanse us from all wickedness" (1 John 1:9 NLT). The dark stains that have robbed you of a life you could be proud of become the very thing that compel you to pursue a lasting change of heart and mind. To gain the resilience and control to overcome obstacles and keep you doing the right thing requires dedication and the hard work of embracing your recovery. I hope that while you're reading my letter you will find your way back to the *real you*. This is also a guide to help you and your partner heal. Personal healing is hard work—the hardest work you will ever do. For your partner, healing is just as hard, though different. For her, the discovery and disclosure of your actions feels like an explosion with the debris blown in every direction, and she is left not knowing how to put herself and life back together. After you have been caught in your betrayals, secrets, and lies, it will take time and a lot of energy on your part to help her facilitate her healing while working your own recovery program. You should want to stop the undesirable behaviors; otherwise, they will get in the way of the healing process. This is easier said than done, which is why this work takes rigorous commitment. It's a difficult process, but it's well worth the effort to move forward and help your partner heal from the avalanche of your indiscretions.

Sexual addiction can be isolating, causing one to withdraw from social activities, friends, and family. The Bible warns us about this: "It is not good for the man to be alone" (Genesis 2:18). "Two people are better off than one, for they can help each other succeed. If one person falls, the other can reach out and help" (Ecclesiastes 4:9, 10). The challenge of putting off the disingenuous false self is in striving and straining to discover the man you were created to be under all the layers of pain, addiction, and discomfort in your life. As you are *becoming*, you will discover strengths you didn't know you had, as well as the ability to overcome weaknesses. Transforming your heart and mind will make you a courageous man of integrity, one who knows how to walk away from evil and walk the way of a righteous man. We are most vulnerable in our grief and sorrow, yet we will find the courage to discover the truth that sets us free. Recovery is not just about meetings, twelve-step programs, or relapsing; it is more about showing up with courage and believing in the process, and knowing that you are doing the right thing even when you cannot predict the outcome.

As you embark on this journey of recovery and healing, finding the lost parts of you, you will begin to experience freedom from the bondage that trapped you into believing lies. Embrace your recovery, and trust in yourself as you do the work. Only you can choose to have control of your life and be a man with dignity and integrity as you evolve into your new identity. You won't want to return to your old ways after you have experienced what the new you looks and feels like.

The Velveteen Rabbit tells us that those who break easily are not the overcomers who endure life's trials. Going through trials and tribulations of this nature can feel like a tornado spiraling out of control, but trials teach us what redemption looks like when we can accept, learn, and grow through them—instead of running from ourselves and using countless coping behaviors to cover the pain. Developing endurance in suffering, without groaning or complaining, will help us find our new selves and redeem what was lost. What we become in the process of *becoming* reflects the work it costs to shed the old and embrace the new.

Consider the art of Kintsugi, an old Japanese method of repairing broken and shattered pottery bowls with gold and silver. The cracks are filled with precious gold, which adds beauty to the sharp and broken edges. After the repair, the bowl is more beautiful and valuable than before *because* of the work and value of the repair. This is a beautiful metaphor for the redemption possible in your life. We can never be beyond restoration and reparation from our brokenness or addictions.

The damaged self needs a refining furnace to remove the impurities of the unwanted behaviors that have hurt you and others along the way. It requires a sincere brokenness and a willingness to do the work of repairing the wreckage in our lives. *Becoming real* requires tolerating discomfort even when your natural inclination is to quit. By choosing a less traveled path, you break new ground to make way for changes in your life. It's like taking a jackhammer to a hardened heart and watching it crack, crumble, and dissolve the inner and outer walls. It's about rearranging your life to rid yourself of the undesirable behaviors that took control of you and stole the love and peace you once had for yourself and others.

This journey is not for the man who is contemplating his next hit. It's for the man who makes a choice to put away the old and embrace the new. This change not only impacts your process of *becoming*, but also matters to the people in your life that have been affected by your choices. You will become the man you know you are and want to be. You will have the integrity to do the right thing for yourself, others, and God.

There will be days, amid decisions to repair and help your partner heal, when you will need to revisit your heart condition and intention to change. You may want to convince yourself that the work is too much: *"This is too hard, I can't change, I can't be what she needs me to be, I am not enough."* But this is your new reality: don't even entertain the idea of giving up—not *today*, not *ever*. You deserve better. She deserves better.

Giving up and walking away will only bring a new set of problems. This journey is transforming, and transformation is necessary for a change of heart. Remember it is the incremental movements that matter for a lasting change. Your partner will also be making changes. Look for them, be attentive, and give credit. Some changes will be small, and others monumental, like asking you to move back home after staying with your parents for the last three months. But mostly, it will be small steps at a time, and these steps will build your confidence and your capacity to live differently. Experiencing the successes and freedom from the bondage that has held its grip on you comes from taking control of your life and not walking in shame.

Understanding Sexual Addiction

The sexual integrity issues I address refer to lack of control over your thoughts and conduct around sexual behaviors and sexual compulsivity. If you picked this book up out of curiosity and concern of whether you have an addiction, this is for you, too. If you are cheating on your partner but do not have a fully developed sex addiction, this could give you an understanding of your behaviors and help prevent that addiction from developing.

The parts of you that have been lost to addiction long to find their way back to your heart. Addiction entices, promising great rewards while tricking you into believing its lies. It's persuasive, telling you that you deserve whatever you want. It seduces you, gripping you with its powerful claws. Does all this sound too familiar? If you have fallen into the stronghold of a sexual addiction, it likely does. Addiction is powerful. It is manipulative, secretive, shaming, devious, and cunning. It is no wonder if you ask yourself: *"How did I let it get so far out of hand?"*

This journey is for the man who wants his life to be better and stronger, in control of his choices, focusing on relationships that matter to him. This man understands that neither he or their partner simply *get over it*; they must go under, over, and through the avalanche that has pummeled their lives. This man is willing to turn himself inside out and go through the process of what it means to walk through the fires, while tearing down the layers of addiction that drives the selfish and prideful path of destruction. If you are this man, make sure you know the road map that leads to a successful journey.

It's important to note that I do not prefer to use the term *sex addict* associated with sexual integrity issues. This term was dated over thirty years ago and has not made it to the Diagnostic and Statistical Manual of

Mental Disorders (DSM-5). I prefer using terms like *"a man in recovery with an intimacy disorder, or sexual integrity issues"*; as far as I am concerned, a man in process of working on his recovery program has a compulsive disorder around sexual thoughts and behaviors, which can sometimes be diagnosed as part of another mental health issue. Yet, I do believe while in the throes of sex addiction behaviors, it is an addiction. Merriam-Webster defines addiction as "a compulsive, chronic, physiological or psychological need for a habit-forming substance, behavior, or activity having harmful physical, psychological, or social effects and typically causing well-defined symptoms (such as anxiety, irritability, tremors, or nausea) upon withdrawal or abstinence: the state of being addicted."[1]

The secrets and lies behind an addiction spread like a deep, open wound that continues to ooze infection to other parts of your mind and body. Slowly and over time, shame becomes a central focus, strips you of important things and relationships that once mattered to you, and convinces you that your actions won't hurt you or anyone. Living a secret double life is exhausting and harder than the pain of change. But I am convinced that change is possible based on my experience working with some of the most wounded and damaged men I've treated. They have done the hard work of putting behind the old, have not given up, and have wanted to make things right. No more compartmentalizing. No more living a double life. They have examined their hearts and rescued themselves from any further and impending destruction. Their lives have been changed forever.

I am a licensed clinician and certified sex addiction specialist. I have been trained to work as a trauma specialist in the areas of Hypnotherapy, Somatic Experience, and Eye Movement Desensitization and Reprocessing (EMDR). I implement all these tools when working with individuals or couples. Most of the men I work with walk into my office with shame and disgust because of what they have done, where they have been, and how they have violated their principles and values and given in to evil. Some are prideful, selfish, and narcissistic. It takes humility and courage to admit what you've done, rather than to stroll in and say, *"She wasn't there for me, she didn't meet my expectations, she cares more about the kids than she does for me, she wouldn't have sex with me, I don't love her anymore."* Regarding your partner's side of things, if there is any ownership on her part, in due time, in her process and healing, she'll own what is hers. But not until you transform your heart and behaviors will she start to trust you again with her heart and feel safe enough to acknowledge behaviors that may have been hurtful on her part. Now, in the early stages of grief and discovery, she will be overcome with grief. If you get stuck in a place thinking you're a victim because of a reaction she's having to something you said or did, you will not give the relationship a chance to repair. You have been the perpetrator and offender, and she is the victim trying to makesense of her new reality from the pain and trauma you have induced by violating your marriage vows.

The men I see in my practice are men who fear losing their partner, family, or job and desperately want to do whatever it takes to get as far away from the secrets and behaviors that have kept them in bondage to sexual sin. Believe it or not, being found out gives you a sense of relief, in some ways. It's exhausting to live in hiding and deceit. Having to cover your steps, forgetting what you said, compartmentalizing, and covering up more lies only nurtures anger and self-righteousness. Men that live like this take on a life of deflecting the truth. This cycle of emotional, verbal, and physical abuse further takes over as a cover-up for the addiction.

I've also trained as a Partner Trauma Specialist, Gottman, and Emotionally-Focused Therapy. Because this type of work is relational, it goes beyond working with the individual with sexual integrity issues. Sexual Addiction is relational trauma. The partner and the relationship need attention to work through the relational trauma and recovery for the healing process.

If you're asking yourself: *"How did my life get so out of control? Why do I do these things, knowing how much they hurt my partner?"* Hang on, keep reading. I hope to bring you some clarity and a better understanding of yourself throughout this letter. You have a lot left in you, don't ever give up on yourself, and you matter way more than you may know.

Trusting God Through Your Trials

I will walk you through the transformation process of *becoming* the person you were meant to be, but only you can choose to walk the journey that will change the narrative of your life.

My relationship with God the Father, the Son, and the Holy Spirit has transformed me into the woman, wife, mother, grandmother, friend, and counselor I am today. I am also the partner of a man who was caught in the trap of pornography. Without my relationship with God, I would not be where I am in life now after all the chaos and mess that traumatized and interrupted my life. I grew up Catholic and appreciate the path it led me on. It gave me an understanding of the Trinity and the Blessed Virgin Mary, and since then I have accepted Jesus as my Lord and Savior.

I have never regretted my decision to give my life to Him. I continue to sin and do things my way more often than I would like; pride and selfishness take precedence over seeking what He would have for me. But thankfully this happens less and less as I grow and mature in Him. The more I know of Him, the less I see of me. I love that the Bible, the Word of Truth, tells me that He will never forsake me. I am humbled by the fact that He is a forgiving God who loves each of us enough to draw us to Himself. He desires to give us his very best no matter what we've done and what our story is.

I make no apologies for the word of God; I speak the truth as I know and understand it. I am not proclaiming to be a theologian; you will come across Scripture in this book, but please don't take offense: I am writing from a place of the heart. The Bible speaks for itself; God's words are transforming, powerful, and life-changing.

Throughout my experiences as a Christian, I have sought to learn and seek Him first, be attentive to what He is directing, guiding and wanting me to learn through the twists and turns of life. I have become introspective, reflective, analytical, and discerning of what God would have for me in trials, triggers, sufferings, and tribulations. Some of my hardest struggles in life have turned into my most profound and teaching moments because they have taught me what it means to fully surrender my heart, life, and commitment to Him. I have learned to turn toward Jesus's heart and become more and more dependent and in love with Him. I know I can't get through life without trials and tribulations, but knowing I have God to comfort and give me the courage and strength I need is where my hope comes from. When I kick and scream, wanting my way, I look and feel just as messy as anyone else who is full of themselves. Left to have it all on my terms has often shown to be destructive. I've learned to trust Him in these difficult moments, knowing He only wants what's best for me.

Being a partner has taught me endurance and patience as I practiced leaning into the unknown and putting my trust in God. Not trusting in my Heavenly Father brought out the darkness that I didn't like about myself, such as, *"I don't need anyone; I can do this on my own, I'm strong; you will never hurt me like this again, you will hurt too, you won't get away with this."* But I know, without a doubt, and choose to believe that He sees me and my heart. I know that only He can heal and transform me, and He is the ultimate comforter. Frederica Mathews-Green, quoted in Peter Scazerro's book, *Emotionally Healthy Spirituality: Day by Day*, speaks to the transformation process in Christ: "God's presence in us is like the fire in the burning bush. It gradually takes us over so that although we remain fully ourselves, we remain the way God originally intended us to be . . . We never lose our identity, but we are filled with God like a sponge is filled with water."[2]

Even if we have different spiritual beliefs, I hope you do not dismiss my letter as another religious farce that leads to nowhere. I don't want you to miss out on something that could be helpful and life-changing in your healing and recovery journey. I don't claim to have any special gift or talent that changes lives, but ask yourself: *"How might my life change if I were transformed and experienced the freedom of becoming the man I am meant to be and not have addiction control me?"*

Before I go any further, *thank you*. I know that you may never get the full depth of your partner's pain, but the fact that you're reading my letter means something to someone somewhere and somehow. You will probably ask yourself, *"What could she know about what it's like for a man to have sexual integrity issues and go through the recovery process?"* As a woman, I can't know the full depth of what it's like for a man to walk through this journey. What I do know is that I've sat with men like yourself, who have been in deep despair, sobbing like children while wishing they could go back in time and change the past, feeling so bad about themselves for hurting their partners and themselves in the way they have. My hope is to come across both as a female therapist and as a friend that cares enough to share my heart in a letter to you. As a partner, I've been on the receiving end of a sexual integrity issue, and as a therapist, I've heard from all aspects of the pain that this addiction induces and have seen the path of destruction it takes on when given full reign. I know that my husband did not intentionally set out to hurt me, and, *if you're holding this book,* I think you might say the same in your situation. My hope is that what I share with you will be helpful from a woman's perspective, as well as a therapist's.

It is my pleasure to walk alongside you in this journey of *becoming*.

Chapter 1

A COMMITMENT TO RIGOROUS HONESTY

"Forgetting the past and looking forward to what lies ahead . . ." Philippians 3:13

The journey through your recovery process will have its ups and down. Most likely, you've not started the recovery process before, but if you have, it's still another opportunity for growth and working through some core issues. I will be giving you step by step directions for recovery. It will be like learning a new culture and language. Personal transformation is required in this new lifestyle. You'll make plenty of mistakes but remember mistakes are an invaluable lesson and an opportunity for growth. Mistakes can be our greatest teachers.

In 2002, I discovered my husband's secrets, lies, compulsive behaviors, and sexual integrity issues, which had been hidden for decades. I was devastated at the discovery. I had no clue, which speaks to how cunning and manipulative compulsive behaviors can be. He kept his secrets for over 30 years of our marriage. He had bouts of being in and out of his addictive behaviors. There were times when I knew something was off with him. I would ask what was happening, and he would lie and deny any part of my suspicions. His lies made me think that I was crazy to even ask. I walked away from these conversations with him feeling confused and ashamed for asking.

There was no more confusion when I found pornography all over the computer, and yet, he swore up and down it wasn't him. This may sound familiar to you if you were caught in the scandal of lies. I was deeply hurt for both of us. For him—because he couldn't share his secrets with me and had held onto them for so long. And for myself, that I had been betrayed and lied to by the man I loved and trusted since I was sixteen years old. I was thankful that he had been found out and the truth was out. It was so daunting; how could I have not known? Was I that stupid that I could not have picked up on it? What other secrets were there? Were there more? Was I not good enough? I felt his remorse and wanted this to go away as much as he did. He couldn't deny it anymore. He came clean and admitted that he had been looking at pornography and lying to me about this issue for years. In a crazy way, it was a relief for both of us. Now we could begin to do the hard work of repairs over the months and years ahead of us. I was thankful for the way we would now talk for hours, exploring what was broken in him, myself, and our relationship. He wanted to understand why he would continue to do these things, knowing it was hurtful to me. He wanted to know more about the core issues that led to his coping mechanism of turning toward pornography.

Sexual addiction is different from other addictions. Drinking alcohol, for example, is socially acceptable; yet, it can also be an addiction, and many of us have a friend or family member who's had treatment for this. A *sex addiction* gets a bigger rap, since there are so many layers of it from pornography to child pornography, prostitution, love addiction, exhibitionism, voyeurism and much more. The fallout of a sex addiction, at its worst, is broken relationships, families torn apart, diseases, and sometimes prison time.

Early on I felt betrayed, abandoned, rejected, alone, and ashamed. I believed I could never be enough compared to the images my husband had examined up close and personal. It crushed my heart and spirit and made me think, *"What parts of him do I know and don't know?"* It's a hard reality that the more you love, the more it hurts, and the longer you love someone, the harder it is to get through the hurt and betrayal. My husband was my first true love; there wasn't anything I wouldn't do for him. I was crazy in love with him. Discovery was a deep cut that reached far into the depths of my heart. *"How could he openly look into my eyes and lie to me?"* I needed time, empathy, understanding, and community with other women whose hearts had been broken, whose lives were torn asunder, and who were in shock: and emotionally fragile. My heart ached and felt like I had been through open heart surgery. I hurt and grieved the loss of the love I believed I knew and was afraid to open up again to a man who for so long could look me straight in the eye and lie.

Some of you might be thinking, *"All men look at pornography,"* or say, *"That's nothing; I've done a lot worse than that."* I get it; skin-to-skin sexual integrity issues are a whole different situation. My heart goes out to the many women whose husbands have been with prostitutes, visited massage parlors, had sex with minors, had sex with men, and much more.

Those realities are devastating and traumatizing for these women. Some leave their marriages, and others try hard to stay, forget, forgive, and move forward. But for many of the women that stay, there isn't a day she isn't reminded of her broken heart. Only time and support can heal and soften the intensity of the pain. However they do it, they move on as best as they can. But there is a scar that will last a lifetime and always hurt. Many will feel tainted no matter what they do. If they do leave, the past impacts their future relationships, making it hard to start over and trust again.

I am not minimizing the pain and trauma for the women whose husband's issues around sexual integrity are *just* pornography and masturbation. It all hurts. The underlying issues for each man going through this are similar, no matter how they are expressed. You will read about all kinds of sexual integrity issues and the impact on the heart, mind, and body in this letter. I want you to understand the trauma and the loss of the reality she once knew and how you can help her heal. We will also talk about shame, but it is important to know early on that when you are in a place of shame, it will only get in the way of helping her heal and the focus you need to work a healthy recovery program.

My work was affected; I thought that not only as a wife, but as a therapist, I should have seen this coming. How could I help anyone else when my marriage was suffering? What was wrong with me? And yet, I knew that his issue with pornography wasn't about me, and I refused to take any blame for that. I had not brought this into our marriage and knew nothing of my husband's addiction before we were married. I knew of his early traumas and could certainly empathize with what it must have been like to be forced out of his childhood home. His dad was a wounded vet from World War II, unable to work, and had post-traumatic stress disorder. His mother worked her fingers to the bone raising a large family. There was emotional and physical abandonment by his dad. As a child, he would cry himself to sleep, longing for love and attention. Unfortunately, at a young age he found his dad's magazine stash; it filled the gap left by loneliness, boredom, and childhood wounds. These wounds will be discussed more in a later chapter.

The more we talked about our childhood losses and trauma, his actions started to make sense to me in a new and different way. I truly cared and felt sorry for the things he went through and the trauma he went through growing up. It didn't excuse his behavior but made a whole lot of sense as to why and how he turned to what he did. Pornography was comforting as a young boy, and it was an invitation to comfort in times of stress and feelings of abandonment as an adult. He is a man with many victories in his life. as a young boy he experienced the thrill of being a wrestling champion, winning all the meets. He got to compete at state but only remembers how lonely he felt getting off the bus alone and walking home in tears as he carried his trophy. No one was there to cheer him on or to celebrate him. Unfortunately, this story and the feelings of loneliness and abandonment are far too familiar to the hurting men and women that have found comfort in the lure of a sex addiction.

My husband was a junior in college studying civil engineering and I was nineteen when we got married. I put him through school while working as a hairstylist. We accepted Jesus as Lord of our lives soon after we were married. We both wanted to study the Bible, and together we enrolled in a Bible college for one year. We loved studying the word of God together. Dan continued his studies in Bible for another two years in the Chicago area while I was home with our babies, learning what it meant to be a Christian, a wife, a mother, and a Bible student.

The church expected Dan to take on leadership, but Bible college does not prepare you to teach Sunday School, lead a small group, work, do home projects, and be a husband and family man, *all at once*. While all that was going on I tended to our family and home. Life got difficult and exhausting for both of us. In doing good things for the church, we lost sight of our vision and mission to grow in Christ and be more like Him. I'm not putting blame on the church for our setbacks. I wish we could have been strong enough to say no to some of the church related requests that took a lot of Dan's time away from his family. We needed that time to grow in the knowledge and principles of the word of God and raise our family. The stress of being overworked in all directions, physically and mentally, over time led to my husband's demise and fall back to his coping strategies with pornography. His addiction came with guilt and shame and kept him from showing up and being honest, while hiding the deepest parts of himself.

Helping Your Partner Heal

If you have just revealed your sexual integrity issues to your partner, she will be experiencing a deep grief and loss of a reality she thought she knew. Your partner needs all of you to be there for her—emotionally, physically, and spiritually. Because of the trauma inflicted in the aftermath of betrayal, you can't afford to miss an opportunity to help and make amends as quickly as possible. Later in the book, I will introduce you to an amends matrix, developed by Jason Martinkus in his book *Worthy of Her Trust*. It's a great read and a great way to make a thorough repair.

Your partner experiences trauma symptoms that disorient her and most men are not equipped to help regulate their partner's disoriented mind and dysregulated body, as well as understand how her body holds trauma and is easily triggered. Unfortunately, it's hard enough controlling and containing yourself when your partner is dysregulated. In most cases, it does not go well unless you take the time to help and understand yourself to understand her and her trauma symptoms.

In those early months of discovery, my husband was not able to be there for me like I needed him to be he went into the *shame tank* and had little to offer me in terms of support. Shame robs us of a fully equipped mind, body, and spiritual integration. This is true of most reactions when caught in lies and deception; the gut reaction is to move away because, as Curt Thompson said, shame is the "leveraging effect that anticipates abandonment."[3]

I am telling you these things because your partner desperately needs you to allow her to grieve and that includes sitting in the loss and trauma with her. The many phases of grief include her anger and bargaining with herself to stay or leave. She is trying to make sense of her new reality. It's crazy-making for her; she has most likely not ever experienced a relational rupture in her adult life with a significant other. In the aftermath of this fracture, she needs to know that she's got control of something. She needs to know you can be there for her, grieve with her, cry with her, and know you won't minimize or shame her for having feelings and a reaction to her pain. She wants to know that you will do your best to build trust. Love her, be patient and kind, and humbly accept her and where she is at in her pain. In some of my worst moments, I said things to my husband I didn't know were in me and did things I never thought I would do. Most of us are not trained or prepared to know exactly what to do in moments like that. It's hard to see someone in the reaction of their trauma, especially when you know you're the cause of it. There isn't anything about this process that is easy. But believe me when I say she desperately wants to know that you can take the hits and face them head-on without running in the other direction. What she is saying is, *"Show me what you're made of—do you love me? Are you big enough to handle me now?"* But you can't do this part on your own; you can't be there for her in a helpful, loving, and empathic way without the help and support of others. It's an illusion to believe you don't need help. You may have kept secrets on your own, but you only need to look at where and how it landed to know it didn't work so well.

You need the companionship of mature brothers who have walked this path and a counselor who has expertise and training in sexual addiction and trauma. It is essential to have several close men who can hold you accountable. These would be men with whom you can trust your heart and thoughts. This, too, will take time; something many of us are uncomfortable with. It takes practice, patience, and rigorous honesty with yourself and the help of accountability partners.

Your partner also needs help and support, but it requires you to take the initiative. Although you are hurting and overcome by shame, you are the wounder, and she needs you to take up your armor and be a soldier willing to fight for her and the marriage. Please don't leave her on the battleground bleeding and wounded by herself. In Doug Weiss's DVD *Helping Her Heal*, he explains that many men's response to their partner's pain is like shooting her with an Uzi gun, and while she's on the ground bleeding, you're complaining about how you hurt your finger. Weiss states that until you understand the pain and trauma that you caused, she will always desperately want to be understood. She wants you to know the pain she is in. Weiss says, "She needs you to stand under her and hold the weight of what she can barely hold. "[4] Getting caught is shameful and humbling, and those feelings can certainly be overwhelming. However, with practice, consider these times that are out of your comfort zone as an opportunity for growth and teachable moments. Tell her you are willing to learn and do what it takes to help her heal.

The marriages that have endured and grown through the pain and suffering in this process of healing and recovering are the ones that have gone deep into the depths of their own pain and emotional injuries. They have looked at why, when, where, and how the traumatized self was traumatized. Patrick Carnes states, from an ongoing project started in the '80s, that the likelihood of an abuse history while working with sex addicts was astounding. His findings show that 81% of sex addicts had experienced sexual abuse; 72% had experienced physical abuse; and 97% had experienced emotional abuse.[5]

I trust that you will choose to help yourself in order to help your partner. Many find it too difficult to stay in this battleground with their partners, especially while facing their own battles. *"I can't do enough for her; I'll never be what she wants or needs me to be; I can't stand to see her hurt so much."* But you can choose differently now than when you were in the throes of your addiction. You were not the man you are today, nor the man you are transforming into. The in-between work matters: you don't get to be the man who experiences freedom, change, love, and forgiveness without all the effort and exertion it takes to "become, it takes a long time, that's why it doesn't happen to people who break easily."[6]

It may be exhausting sometimes, but you are capable of the ongoing transformation that is required for radical change. Remember that change is step-by-step, and each step matters. Your efforts make a difference in the here and now as transformation occurs. Wherever you are in your process matters; turn those difficult moments around for a teachable, life-changing moment that matters in the long run.

It is difficult for some partners to stay; they are so afraid of getting hurt again. To open their hearts and believe you, trust you, and simultaneously wrap their minds around the discovery and disclosure. It can take months, years, and even more than that. It also can depend on whether she has had other traumas in her life around sex, abuse, and betrayal. Whether she stays or not, do your own work, be the best you can be, and doing the work will change you inside and out.

I want to encourage you in your current state to know yourself, be a student of self, and be known to others as you integrate new and old discoveries in this incredible journey of *becoming*, embracing the pain of recovery, and helping her heal.

You Are Worthy of Forgiveness

I would like to say a word to the man reading this letter that has accepted Jesus as Lord and Savior; perhaps you never fully understood what that meant for you. Maybe you are curiously asking, *"Why would God forgive someone like me?"* Whoever you are, wherever you are in your walk with Him, Jesus took our sins and made us right before God as He hung on the cross. He gave us eternal life and made a covenant to take away our sins. "For everyone, from the least to the greatest, will know me already . . . And I will forgive their wrongdoings, and I will never again remember their sins" (Hebrews 8:11-12).

We have all rebelled against God's word in one way or another. You matter to God; He has cleansed us of all unrighteousness and wants us to experience the grace He offers that sets us free from the bondage we carry. When we ask for forgiveness of our iniquities, He remembers them no more. You are forgiven! My prayer for you is that you live in the grace and knowledge of His word.

I am reminded of Joe, a friend of mine, who has a difficult time accepting that God loves him as he is, imperfect and flawed, as we all are. Joe struggles with forgiveness and will tell you that all he deserves are the crumbs that are dropped under the table. He thinks he is a wretched man for some of the things he has done. We were studying the Bible together, and he shared how he related to the Old Testament character Mephibosheth in the book of Samuel. When a shepherd boy named David, whom the prophet Nathan had prophesied would later become king of the Israelites, was anointed, the current king, Saul, was afraid. He tried in many ways to kill David, to avoid the prophecy from coming true. But Saul's son, Jonathan, was David's best friend. When Jonathan got wind of his father's schemes, he warned David and told him to flee for his life. These two young men had a covenant with each other.

Later, both Jonathan and Saul were killed fighting the Philistines at the battle of Mount Gilboa. Jonathan's young son, Mephibosheth, was taken into hiding to protect him from the incoming king, David. In the escape, Mephibosheth was injured and became lame in both feet.

But many years later, David remembered his friend's kindness and sought to honor Jonathan. He inquired about Jonathan's family: "Is anyone still alive from Saul's family? If so, I want to show kindness to them" (2 Samuel 9:3). When Mephibosheth was brought to David, the king, he bowed down in fear of him.

David said, "Don't be afraid! I intend to show kindness to you because of my promise to your father Jonathan" (2 Samuel 9:7).

Mephibosheth couldn't hear this or take this in. He said, "Who is your servant, that you should show such kindness to a dead dog like me?" (vs. 8)

David welcomed Mephibosheth back to the royal court and gave him a place of honor, returning to him all the lands that had belonged to his grandfather Saul and providing servants to care for him.

I had never read this story before, and I was intrigued as to how Joe could say he only deserved the crumbs, since the end of the story ended with favor and royalty for Mephibosheth. Why couldn't he see that he deserved that same favor himself and live with the promise of redemption? Instead, he believed the lies he heard of himself as a child: *"You're no good; you'll never amount to anything, no one could love you, you're a failure."* Throughout our adult lives many of us continue to believe the lies and hurtful messages we heard as children, and have a difficult time forgiving ourselves for things we have done; the lies are damaging and challenging to overcome.

When my friend Joe read the story Mephibosheth aloud (2 Samuel 9), he cried and truly believed he didn't deserve anything better. His wife gently put her hand on his arms and said, *"David the King invited him to his table and treated him as one of his sons; you don't have to eat the crumbs."* That evening, as we gathered around our sweet friend, I pulled out a crown and robe I had in a costume pile, and we crowned our friend Joe with love. You, too, are robed in righteousness. You have been forgiven—no matter what you've done. He, our great God, is merciful and cleanses us from all unrighteousness. Joe still struggles to grasp this truth; he has to remind himself that he has been forgiven and has a gracious God who wants him to experience victory. We all deserve another opportunity to distinguish right from wrong and correct the wrong.

I've talked to men in tears with a repentant heart about the damage they've done, and the shame they feel about dishonoring their relationship with God, not knowing how to restore and rebuild what they believe is unforgivable. Don't let the evil one play havoc with your mind; all things and people are forgivable to God. If you can get to a place where you ask forgiveness of your sins, "He is faithful and just to cleanse . . . you from all unrighteousness" (1 John 1:9). Asking and accepting His forgiveness is essential in putting on the armor of God and fighting off the enemy. Acknowledging our sins and weaknesses is a first step, and as a Christian, I am thankful that I have personally experienced God's grace and forgiveness. Furthermore, I am better equipped to be there for others. "He comforts us in all our troubles so that we can comfort others. When they are troubled, we will be able to give them the same comfort God has given us." (2 Corinthians 1:4).

Let's meet Bob for a moment: Bob's sexual integrity issues were hidden for many years and the pain he caused his wife through *"sexual sin"* and lies was a lot for her to process. He came to therapy in search of answers, healing, and a path to forgiveness. As he began to heal, Bob also began to understand what it means to be aligned to God's will, experience remorse and seek forgiveness, and then accept forgiveness for himself. In a letter to his wife, Bob laid out a heartfelt apology:

> *"I am sorry that I broke your trust and broke our marriage vows to you by having these relationships. I am truly sorry that I did not focus my attention on you, our marriage, and our family as much as I should have because of these relationships."*[7]

Bob's letter continued to outline the shame he feels for his behaviors and the regret he has for breaking his partner's trust and their marital vows. He also acknowledges the progress he's made in healing and his hopes to align his life with God's will and to lean into biblical guidance: *"I have focused hard on being the man God wants me to be. I have committed to God to be the man He wants me to be."* Bob took a long, hard look at the condition of his heart. He was filled with shame for his *"disgusting and degrading behaviors."* He understood that when you don't follow through on a promise to God, your spouse, and yourself, there is a break, a disunity, and a disconnection from your heart to God's heart. God takes joy when we acknowledge our sins, because "He is faithful . . . to forgive us and cleanse us" (1 John 1:9).

I so appreciate how Bob owned up to his indiscretions: *"While I lied to myself, suggesting it is natural and part of being a man to act out, I have known it was wrong, which is why I feel so ashamed. I know my behaviors are not aligned with God's will for me."* It's between you and God to make it right. As a Christian, I understand I can do nothing to earn His merit. Jesus paid the price at the cross for my sins, and only when I get to a place where I am understanding what my sinful behaviors mean to Him, and hurtful to myself and others, can I truly ask for His forgiveness. He cleanses me from all unrighteousness. The cleansing process is meant to teach us to do what is right.

> *"All scripture is inspired by God and is useful to teach us what is true and to make us realize what is wrong in our lives. It corrects us when we are wrong and teaches us to do what is right. God uses it to prepare and equip his people to do every good work."* 2 Timothy 3:16-17

I treat and see each man who walks into my office respectfully, as a human who deserves the right to heal, gather information, and make choices for himself. I will walk you through the protocol of what it looks like to disclose your story, learn how to love yourself, love the significant people in your life, address your hurts and abuse, and learn the trauma model to help her heal in the aftermath of your sexual integrity issues.

If you are on board, hang in there. I want to help you heal as much as I want to help you help her heal. I want you to be successful, as you both deserve it!

Understanding Her Pain

The women I work with desperately want their men to feel their pain and take it away. Some of the men in my couple's groups say things such as, *"I wish I had known this stuff; it could have made such a difference from the get-go of our recovery and healing process."* Your partner matters, and what you say and do matters now and in the future.

When your wife discovered your sexual integrity issues, she was blindsided in all directions. It felt to her like an 18-wheeler had run over her. She could barely breathe and catch her breath. The discovery of your indiscretions put her in shock, bleeding out, wounded emotionally, physically, and spiritually. She needed and still needs you to be there to help put her back together from the shock and trauma of discovery. She needs you to shield her from the shattered memories of the past, lies, secrets and deceit you kept from her. She wanted to wake up and believe this was a bad dream. At the same time, she doesn't want to wake up from the aftermath of the sharp shards that remind her of the pain she is in.

After feeling enough guilt and shame over his addiction, Mark walked into the kitchen and suddenly disclosed to his wife Janna that he had been with prostitutes and going to strip clubs and massage parlors. Out of desperation from the guilt and shame, and wanting to end his life, he called a treatment center and left for help. He left and Janna was there gasping for air on the floor where she had collapsed. Broken beyond measure, she lay there in a fetal position throughout the night, unable to move or sleep.

Mark had gone for help and left no information for any contact. She had no clue where he was or how long he would be gone. She was in shock and suffered severely from the trauma of her new reality. It made no sense to her as she tried to grasp what had happened. She managed to find me online, and we set up an appointment as soon as possible. I kept her on the phone as long as possible while reviewing some basic details for her safety, yet she could barely take in what I was saying. Janna was hardly able to slow down and breathe. *"Just one at a time, just one breath at a time,"* I was saying, as she was hyperventilating telling me her story.

I called a sweet sister and partner to invite Janna to a fellowship of partners who had walked down a similar path. I would see Janna at her worst, shaking, sobbing, and barely able to say anything through her tears. She repeated, *"What am I going to do? I can't eat or sleep, and I have a child to take care of,"* as she rocked back and forth.

Her husband did the right thing by getting help. He knew he could not continue with the level of betrayal and addiction that led from one prostitute to another. But he was not able to face the agony that he was about to see his wife go through as he disclosed more of his indiscretions. It was cowardly; he shrunk in the face of devastation and the challenge of helping her heal. Very few men disclose on their own, as he did; he deserves credit for that. He eventually returned from the treatment center three months later. There was minimal contact with him while he was at the center.

The repair was extremely difficult, as you can imagine, with all the trauma that comes from abandonment, along with leaving her to pick up all the pieces left undone and putting her in a position to do the clean-up on her own. While Mark was convicted of what he had done and committed to getting help, he had too much guilt and shame to honor his marital covenant at that time. He did not stay to help Janna through the early discovery stages. She needed safety and security, help with chores, family and work, and someone to take over while she got support and counseling. When you take ownership and start the road to recovery, you make a statement to honor yourself and your partner's pain. You are saying, *"I did this. I caused your broken heart, I betrayed you, and I take full responsibility for what I've done. I will do whatever is needed and possible on my behalf to be the husband I should have been to you."*

In the book *The Cry of the Soul*, Dan Allender and Tremper Longman capture the essence of how dealing with our emotions in these hard circumstances can lead us to God: "Ignoring our emotions is turning our back on reality; listening to our emotions ushers us into reality. And the fact is where we meet God. Emotions are the language of the soul. They are the cry that gives the heart a voice . . . We forget that change comes through brutal honesty and vulnerability before God."[8]

Five years after finding evidence of Tony's betrayals, Suzanne reports that if Tony had not been able to endure some of her most challenging moments, she would not have stayed. This couple went through the process of rigorous honesty and speaking the truth in love, even when it hurt. Suzanne was in so much emotional pain that she could barely exist. She would fall on the floor into a fetal position. Tony and I would get her on the couch in my office, and I would do touch therapy while teaching him how to help her be in the here and now—a place she didn't want to be because her new reality was so painful. I would gently put both hands on her temples and move my hands around to her shoulders and hands. I constantly checked in with her, asking if she was all right with the touch. If you try this and have a partner who does not want you to touch her, be respectful; ask if there's anything you can do, bring her some ice, and stay nearby. Please don't go away; she wants you to know how much she's hurting. Not all partners experience the trauma as Suzanne did but can probably relate to her experience. It is her new reality and yours as well. Stay, don't run. You need to stay present, and work at getting better at that; don't allow shame to take over and shut you down.

Giving in to shame will only keep the pretense and the mask on. It will hold you to the dark side that prevents your genuine, authentic self from helping her heal. If that's the case, you're setting yourself up for more failures and losses. Just look at the destruction you've already experienced in your life. If you refuse to do the work, you will remain trapped as a prisoner held in bondage to lies and deceit. You must be rigorously honest with yourself, God, and your partner. Honesty is a building block that ensures a foundation for acceptance and loving yourself and others. You now have the freedom to be free from the grips of shame. You are allowing yourself the experience of redemption in exchange for the agony of what evil wants to destroy in you. Rediscovering who you are without the wide range of setbacks while overcoming addiction is freedom and peace worth fighting for.

This doesn't mean your partner will notice, acknowledge or give you kudos for all your efforts. You can't expect to be praised or acknowledged for doing the right thing; if that's what you're looking for, you will be disappointed and defeated. The new behaviors you are putting on and the way you manage your life now is what she expected from you when she committed to being in a relationship with you.

She will consistently hurt. This kind of pain doesn't go away on its own, and she has mending and work to do as well. Think of this as a medical emergency. She's had open-heart surgery. Be patient; she's recovering. Throw your expectations out the door. I have heard way too many times, *"Why isn't she further along?"* She needs time and patience. Give her the time she needs. She so wishes she could feel the freedom you have from the sexual integrity issues, if you are no longer acting out. But that sense of freedom cannot be rushed.

The intensity of the pain subsides as she gets stronger and more courageous in her healing process. The frequency of the triggers that throw her back into the trauma slows down in due time. And in due time she notices and says: *"Hey, it's been a few days that I have not dwelt on his infidelities or thought about what my husband has done with other women."* That is a great victory for her. Also, her discovery is still fresh compared to the time you spent acting out, and she is now just discovering it. Be patient and endure with love and kindness; it will grow you.

Transformation is a genuine conversion of the old you into the man you were meant to be.

> *"That means that anyone who belongs to Christ has become a new person. The old life is gone, a new life has begun! And all this is a gift from God, who brought us back to Himself through Christ. And God has given us this task of reconciling people to him. For God was in Christ, reconciling the world to Himself, no longer counting men's sins against them."* 2 Corinthians 5:17-19

Your First Task: Find a Group

One of the first assignments I give to the men I work with is to find a group where you can get support to start and stay on the path of recovery. It's so crucial to your healing to have the feeling of belonging to a brotherhood. You need a safe place to be with like-minded men who want to have a change of heart. The men standing in the battleground, who are faithful and honest with their partners in their recovery process, experience personal and relational success. They are men who can be trusted: dependable and predictable. They are men who are working on loving themselves and learning how to love their wives—men who encourage one another to stay on the right and narrow path; men who own and take this *becoming* seriously are living a shame-free life and are experiencing success.

You can turn your life around with the help of a team there to cheer you on in the good times and sit with you in moments of despair. The team is there to help you stay grounded and press on to the values and principles that align with your heart. The team is not there to keep you in defensiveness, denial, or blame. I love the stories I hear about calling each other out of the darkness and into the light.

Some men aren't ready to start their recovery journey. John would show up at his recovery group, reporting over and over that he had lost his sobriety, all the while not paying attention to the group's advice for a different path. I, too, as his counselor, had been giving him the same advice: *"John, driving to work would be better than taking the train,"* I would say, *"It's too easy for you to fall back into your addiction."* John's issue was frotteurism; he would excitedly scan the train car for the pretty women and sit right up close enough to touch her legs or hips.

The group finally asked him to leave since their own sobriety was in jeopardy. They were triggered by his behavior, and it wasn't easy to hear John's story week after week, putting them in a position where their own fantasies could easily be set off. The group asked him to leave and come back when he was ready to commit to his sobriety and work his program.

Unfortunately, I also made the difficult decision to let him go as a client. Until he was ready to commit to the work it takes to be sober, it wasn't fair to the brothers, and I thought it was a waste of his time and his money to show up each week for counseling without the effort to work on his recovery and underlying issues.

In contrast to John, Ben was guarded, unaware of his emotions and vulnerabilities, and an extreme people pleaser. His dad wanted him to follow in his older brother's footsteps, choose a career that supports a family, and play it safe. This led to an upper management job after his college career. However, while he was in college, he partied hard, binge drank, and developed a pornography addiction. He married Felicia, and these behaviors were well hidden. Years later, when he got caught, Felicia discovered his stash in a hidden corner of the closet, and he was forced to tell her about his addiction to pornography. Over time, Ben's recovery program took on a new and personal meaning. Ben would say, *"I don't know how I got here; I come from a good family; my parents did a good job raising all of us kids."*

We delved into his family of origin wounds and the repeated patterns that kept him from understanding how *"playing it safe"* kept him from being true to himself. Telling others what he thought they wanted to hear and doing what they expected of him cost him a lot of losses by not being his true self. His pornography addiction was a coping mechanism that took him into a fantasy world and the illusion of having control of his life. He missed out on his true dream of being an artist, which could have had great potential for him. He wasn't practiced at making decisions independently; it was easier and not so risky to do what others thought he should do. If things didn't turn out as he hoped, he could secretly blame others and not own up to his flaws and lack of ownership. It wasn't until

Ben made the effort to be known to himself and the brotherhood that his recovery work started to matter from a change of heart. He admitted to himself and others his weaknesses and failures and made a point to remember his intentions to be true to himself.

Don't Give Up; Keep Going

You know you are moving in the right direction when there is something, even a small part, inside of you that is motivating you to do the right thing. For this, I commend you. Stick to the task, don't stray, and you will get to a place of healing in due time. Some experts say it takes up to five years to recover; focus on one step at a time. Don't compare yourself to others. You don't start this journey and arrive in five years. You are moving towards healing; while the pendulum goes back and forth, signs of progress and setbacks converge to the energy, wisdom, knowledge, and good sense needed for a deeper understanding and growth of oneself. Press on.

A verse to memorize—to help you get through moments of defeat:

> *"We now have this light shining in our hearts, but we ourselves are like fragile clay jars containing this great treasure. This makes it clear that our great power is from God, not from ourselves. We are pressed on every side by troubles, but we are not crushed. We are perplexed, but we are not driven to despair. We are hunted down, but never abandoned by God. We get knocked down, but we are not destroyed. Through suffering, our bodies continue to share in the death of Jesus so that the life of Jesus may also be seen in our bodies."*
>
> 2 Corinthians 4:7-10

Your partner will see changed behaviors when you're constantly and consistently working on your program. This effort also translates into a trust that you are rebuilding with her; even if she doesn't notice the change of heart and behaviors and you don't hear her affirmation, do not give up on yourself or the hope of restoration. She will sense any lies, deceit, or manipulation. She has an even stronger sense of intuition now. She wants to believe you and hopes that this glorious light and power given to you by God will lead you and you won't give up and quit. We are called to live by the spirit of the living God.

Remember the words that Paul wrote to the Galatians:

> *"So I say, let the Holy Spirit guide your lives. Then you won't be doing what your sinful nature craves. The sinful nature wants to do evil, which is just the opposite of what the Spirit wants. And the Spirit gives us desires that are the opposite of what the sinful nature desires. These two forces are constantly fighting each other, so that you are not free to carry out your good intentions. But when you are directed by the Spirit, you are not under obligation to the law of Moses. When you follow the desires of your sinful nature, the results are very clear: sexual immorality, impurity, lustful pleasures, idolatry, sorcery, hostility, quarreling, jealousy, outbursts of anger, selfish ambition, dissension, division, envy, drunkenness, wild parties, and other sins like these."* Galatians 5:16-21

God's word is clear, giving us direction and the course of our lives. Living according to God's plan, I believe, makes us much better human beings in all aspects of our lives.

You have a lot going on in your recovery, and relationally, you must know without a shadow of a doubt that rigorous honesty and empathy will help her heal. A vision for recovery and healing pursues a healthy, sober future as you navigate what you need to make empowering choices. Abandoning old behaviors and thoughts by replacing them with a new heart, renewed self, and new relationships will lead to the development of the committed true self.

QUESTION FOR YOUR HEART

Are you willing to commit to your recovery process? How might it make a difference for you?

Chapter 2

DISCLOSURE

> "'Can a man hide in secret places so I cannot see him?'
> declares the Lord. 'Do I not fill heaven and earth?'"
>
> Jeremiah 23:24

In this chapter, I talk about the formalities of having a Formal Therapeutic Disclosure (FTD). You will learn step-by-step after agreeing as a couple to the guidelines and protocol a disclosure takes you through. You will learn what it means to hold fast, under the hardships, failures, and successes one experiences while persevering through a therapeutic disclosure.

Hebrews 12:1 says, "Let us strip off every weight that slows us down, especially the sin that so easily trips us up. And let us run with endurance the race God has set before us." Getting through a formal therapeutic disclosure takes steadfastness, focus, and endurance. You will build a community that supports the hard work you are doing to regain trust and rebuild what has been ruptured and traumatized in the aftermath of a sex addiction.

When a couple comes to my office for the FTD process, I explain the logistics of a disclosure: the timeline, purpose, and commitment required to work through the process. More importantly, I tell the couple to think and pray about this process. Most couples that have been through it are thankful for the opportunity to be entirely truthful and transparent. Moving forward, vulnerability and truth become the new norm. They acknowledge that an honest disclosure is putting the past behind them to move forward as part of the necessary work for healing and recovery. It's not about forgetting the past but moving ahead with rigorous honesty.

For the betrayed partner, the infamous question is, *"Is there more?"* Most women will say they want to believe they have been given a complete disclosure before and at discovery—but that's not always the case.

New information often comes up in the FTD, which is one reason I don't do disclosures in a one or two-hour session. It often takes months to prepare a formal disclosure, for both her sake and yours. Remember that any new information you reveal but have known about for years is fresh and new to her. You're doing this to build trust and empathy. Considering her needs and trauma, while she is taking this information in, it's important to go at this gently and not rush it.

Women hear from other women, *"Why would you go through this process? Why would you stay? He's only going to do it again!"* And this is just a fragment of what she's hearing and going through; all the while, she's trying so hard to see the good in you and believe in this process, and she wants to know that you are telling her the whole truth. She deserves the truth. She hasn't gone anywhere; she's still with you, hoping for the best outcome through the entire process.

There are steps to follow, and following them provides a sense of reassurance and structure for both of you. If you sign up for this, you can't do it with reservations; you have to go into this with nothing to hide. When we agree with the timeframe and the protocol has been set up, we press forward with the FTD. From the start of writing to the actual disclosure day, it could be two to four months. It's not a quick-done deal; many variables must be discussed and planned. Be as specific as you need to: Do we drive in together or separate cars? Do you have a self-care plan after disclosure? Who will be your support people? On disclosure day, you take a deep breath, put aside any defensiveness, read your disclosure and answer any new questions that may and could show up, aside from the questions she's put together and expects to be answered at disclosure. If any clarification is needed, we slow down and attend to it.

Most likely, as you're writing your disclosure, you're still living with your partner, and she is trying to be patient while waiting for a disclosure. Disclosures can be delicate and need to be handled that way. While your partner wants the truth and nothing of the lies and secrets, she will tell us how much and how little of the details and information she wants. I not only guide the work throughout the process but there are moments we will need to slow down the process as she tries to catch her breath. We wait, sometimes in silence, until she is ready to keep going. Her thoughts and emotions are often all over the place. She is like a scared little puppy. She is working hard to pay attention and doesn't want to miss a word.

Why Disclose?

You disclose for many reasons, including health risks, which can be life or death. It is challenging for most wives to get over that a spouse would not have used protection at their expense, putting them at risk of a fatal disease, such as HIV, Hepatitis C (which is transmitted sexually or via dirty needles), human papillomavirus (HPV), as well as many other sexually transmitted diseases (STDs). This can be a deal breaker in a marriage.

Generally, as your partner starts to write her questions out for you to answer on disclosure day, they may feel endless: *"Were you ever with a minor? Did you molest or assault a child? Did you ever involve children in any way? Were you with a prostitute? Did you use protection?"* These are hard questions for her to ask, and she hopes her intuition is off. It's a continuing battle for her. It's like the after-effect of open-heart surgery in an unconscious and conscious state, barely breathing and trying to heal from the surgery.

Behaviors that are illegal or put the partner's health or the finances of a household at risk make the timeliness of disclosure even more important. Matters are complicated even further by the age of children, the state of finances and health, years invested in the marriage, and, in some cases, children born out of your infidelity.

If you are reading this letter, and have not had a therapeutic disclosure, and are still holding secrets, I encourage you to seek help from a trained and certified sex addiction therapist to know how to help your partner and yourself through this difficult time. Do not postpone the inevitable; you deserve the freedom a therapeutic disclosure can offer.

Commit to Telling the Whole Truth

You can go through a disclosure process, not be rigorously honest, and not be working a healthy recovery program. You can hold back and not fully disclose, but I tell you this: *it will catch up to you.* Your partner is no fool; she knows what she knows and feels what she feels now that she knows what she knows. This process is about trust-building and allowing you to prove you can be a trustworthy man with integrity.

Megan's husband read his disclosure in a timeline and noticed that he had been with a prostitute while they were on vacation in the North Carolina Mountains.

"Was this the time we were going through fertility treatments?" she asked. She listened intently and tried to follow the sequence of events while trying to make sense of how this could have happened and asking herself: *"How did I not know or have any clue?"* This is her traumatized brain in a fragile state, trying so hard to sit in on the disclosure as she's remembering the past and trying to make sense of the present. I understand that it is also difficult for you to focus, watch, disclose, and see her reaction to your disclosure. Most men at this juncture just want to skip over any new or especially hurtful parts and read through it as fast as they can. Also, knowing it's tearing her apart and breaking her heart is the last thing you want to do again. I get that!

You may ask, then why? Why go through this and put her through such pain? She wants the truth; she would rather have the truth, than stay in a relationship with you knowing you're still lying to her.

As soon as she starts to feel stronger and begin healing, if there's been any dribbling or staggering of more secrets and information, it can throw her right back into her trauma. And this is why a complete therapeutic disclosure is needed. Otherwise, she starts to get back on her feet after a bit and boom, you disclose something you've held back and she is knocked back down again. It takes the wind out of her. You may have had good intentions to not hurt her by holding back and thinking that giving her bits and pieces is better than all at once, but it doesn't work that way.

In their book *Facing Heartbreak*, Stefanie Carnes, PhD, Mari A. Lee, LMFT, and Anthony D. Rodriquez, LCSW speak candidly about what it looks and feels like when you attempt to "do damage control by initially disclosing only some of the sexual acting out . . . Maria, a fifty-seven year old client, sums it up well, she made this tragic but truthful statement after discovering her husband of twenty-seven years had multiple online-sexual sexual affairs that dated back decades. 'Staggered disclosures destroyed my ability to trust my female intuition, my gut. My husband's constant lies and half-truths about his affairs left me feeling like a worthless shell of a wife. I can't even trust myself any longer.'"[9]

Your partner gets to choose what she wants for her future and in those choices, she can choose to stay or leave. It's a difficult decision and it will take much reflection on her part to determine what she genuinely wants and can live with. She cannot predict the future. She is so tender and broken-hearted, and yet it can be that she sees what you are willing to do to help her heal that makes the difference. Be patient with her and yourself.

She so desperately wants the wounder to take the pain away, to make the nightmare go away. Some women don't have a choice between staying or leaving. It could be a matter of children, finances, or mental and health issues. Whatever the situation is, she has to figure out for herself how to stay or how to leave.

Preparing for Disclosure

Disclosure is a long process and typically I plan three months to prepare for it. It is so difficult for the partner to think of waiting another three months for a disclosure; she's dying inside. Yet most of the women I work with, once they have the information and protocol, are willing to wait. This is a pure act of love and kindness on her part. She is suspending her worst nightmares and allowing you the time and space to work on it and yourself, while she waits for you to present the truth and work you've done.

After going over the details of the FTD, you may be writing and rewriting drafts of your disclosure up to three to four times. You write until we are both in agreement of the truth being told, and how it's written. It can be overwhelming when you start the writing, but you don't want her to think you just threw this together. I recommend three months of preparation because it takes at least that amount of time to write your story. It's like writing her a letter of your life story. Her heart is on the line, and you want her to know you're holding it through the whole process. You should carefully consider her heart and feelings as you write. We set up dates within our three-month timeframe for each draft. I read and review each the content in each draft and how it's presented. You'll address your partner by name in the disclosure/letter. For example, *"Lynn, when you were out of town for your birthday last year, I spent the whole weekend looking at pornography. When we would talk, and you asked me if I missed you, I made up stories of how busy I was. I'm sorry I lied, Lynn; you did not deserve that."*

The first draft is generally the hardest. It might be necessary to mention body parts and it's very important to choose your words carefully. If she hears crass or slang terms, your partner will likely get stuck imagining you with a woman that looks as described. Use the proper word for body parts if you feel you must include them. For example, *"She asked if I would follow her to her office and she'd show me her breasts."* Some partners would rather know that information than not, and it's important to remain respectful to all involved. As part of the process, I invite your partner to write a list of questions she wants you to answer. She may need to know what fetishes you had or have. She and I will discuss the lasting effects of knowing some of these details as we review her questions together.

Once I've gone through your first draft, we move on to the rewrite, the second draft. The men I've worked with on disclosures are patient and trusting of me; they know I want this to go as well as a disclosure of this nature can be. By now their heart is in the right place, they are willing to do the hard work, and are wanting to stop the lies, cheating, etc., to rebuild a new trust and life with their partner.

A disclosure can use the language of the first step of Alcoholics Anonymous (AA), Sexaholic Anonymous (SA), etc.: *"We admitted we were powerless over [sex addiction]-and that our lives had become unmanageable."*[10] The similarity between the first step of AA and disclosure is that you must get real with yourself. You acknowledge you have a problem and that your life has become unmanageable. You are breaking through the cycles of denial, secrets, and lies as you disclose the truth. The stories I often hear start off saying something of this nature: *"At the age of nine, I found the stash of magazines my dad hid in the basement, along with the sex videos I watched as often as I could."* The experts in this field tell us addiction is progressive, involving an increased tolerance to the drug of choice. As you write your disclosure, you may notice even more the progression of your addictive behaviors.

Continue to write and write again until all the secret compartments are emptied out, and the truth is told. I will advise you to do a healthy self-care check-up while you are writing because you will be triggered as you remember some of the details of childhood wounds. You may find yourself dissociating, which is not an unusual coping mechanism with most addictions. It's like amnesia; you disconnect from your feelings, thoughts, and memories. Some of you are writing about situations that you may have never told anyone about, and have done everything and anything to not open that Pandora's box. Our brains shut down and want to protect us from these overwhelming experiences.

If you disassociate while writing the disclosure, here's a model I like to use to bring you back to present:

S.O.S.: Stop, Orient, Scale.

1. While you're writing, **stop** and check in every thirty minutes with yourself.

2. **Orient** using your senses: What do I see, hear, smell, and feel? Feel your feet on the floor; ground yourself.

3. Then, on a **scale** of one to ten, think of your worst experience as a ten and ask yourself, where am I now, in this moment, compared to my worst experience?

If you're around a seven, what needs to happen now to get yourself to a six and a half? Do your check-ins regularly and notice where you started to drift off in your writing. This is essential to bring up with your therapist. You may have to slow the writing down to process what's coming up for you as you think it through and memories show up.

Knowing ourselves is a lifetime journey. It's normal to want to figure out what happened and how we end up with some of our hang-ups and addictions. This is one of the blessings of writing your story. I'm not saying that you will be all figured out and cured once this is over. We grow, mature, and develop throughout our lives. This step opens one door that leads to another. Be a student of self, acquire wisdom and knowledge as you experience what life has for you.

Your men's group, the brotherhood, needs to know you are working on your disclosure. You may need some encouragement as you write the story of your life, given that statistically, most people in your situation have experienced trauma, be it physical, emotional, verbal abuse or abandonment. At the end of a written disclosure, I ask that you report how you will stay *safe*, *sober*, *healthy*, and *honest* in each of these categories: *physically*, *emotionally*, *spiritually*, *intellectually*, and *sexually*. This gives her hope, knowing you have a plan.

The timeline for the disclosure also applies to your partner writing out her questions for you to answer. Her questions are important. I also let her know that knowing the names, places, and positions can leave an imprint in her brain—but it is up to her to decide if she wants them. For example, imagine if you have had sex with a friend of hers and you continued to be in touch as a couple with this woman after disclosure—and sooner or later, she finds out. Think how hurtful and painful it would be for her to discover that she continued to be around this person and now knowing the two of you kept a secret from her. One of the women I worked with had two hundred questions for disclosure, and each question was just as important to her as the twenty to thirty questions another woman might have. The longer the relationship or prior traumas, the more questions she may have. She deserves the truth and wants and needs it for her healing.

Once I have reviewed your partner's questions with her, I will hand them over to you to answer before the official disclosure day. You will then answer her questions on paper before discussing them with me or your therapist. These are mostly open-ended questions, not often *yes or no* questions. I want to know that you went through her questions thoroughly. She will only hear your answers on disclosure day. At disclosure, there is time for clarification if she needs it. There are times I have noticed the partner lagging, trying to make sense of the last few sentences you may have just read, and I will ask if we need to slow down; and of course, she can also take responsibility for herself and ask for what she needs. But I find in moments of lagging, she may be in a trauma response. So much work has gone into this, and we don't want to hurry through it.

To give you a sense of the types of questions partners typically ask, the following are questions that Riley wanted answers to. They are painfully thought out, hard for her to think she would even have to ask, and hard to know the truth. The questions are relentless and, to say the least, exhausting for her.

1. Have you had affairs (unpaid sex)? If so, when? With whom? How long?
2. Have you ever acted out in our camper, specifically asking about the few times you went camping alone?
3. Have you ever had anyone in our home? Where was I? What was I doing? What was going on between us?
4. Have you ever had anyone in our cars? Which ones, and how many times? How many women?
5. When did visiting prostitutes begin, what was going on for you?
6. Have you been with multiple women at once, how did this come about?
7. How many repeat women have you been with, and how many times each and over what time?
8. Have you been with anyone I know? If so, who?
9. I need a listing of all the locations in which you betrayed me so I don't make triggers up in my head.
10. Have you run into women you've acted out with in public places? If so, what have you done about it?
11. What kind of pornography have you watched?
12. Were you ever with Nancy and how far did it get?

Regardless of how painful it feels to be asked questions like these—she hurts badly to even have to ask. Taking the time to answer her questions respectfully and in detail helps to assure her that you're taking this process seriously and you see her pain.

After Disclosure

Writing your disclosure is stressful; your mind is on overdrive trying to remember details that are difficult to bring back to memory. It is not unusual sometime after disclosure that you find yourself remembering things that were not on the disclosure. You have better clarity of mind, and the brain fog has been lifted. For example: *"By the way, I am remembering that I did not include this in my disclosure; at the golf outing I went to with my brother last fall, I got a lap dance from a stripper at the club."* Memories like this may appear as you heal and recover.

Don't dismiss telling her about this new information to avoid causing her more pain. Talk to your therapist and request help on how to share the memories that are now coming up for you. Don't talk yourself into thinking, *"We're in a good spot now, and I don't want to rip open another wound."*

Along this line, let your partner know that if any new information comes to mind in the future, you will disclose it to the best of your knowledge within a certain time frame after processing it with your therapist and possibly your group and accountability person. You may eventually be far enough along in your own recovery and emotional maturity to share without the assistance of others. This would mean that you have learned to regulate yourself and assist your partner when needed in a high-conflict situation. You will learn how to take time outs and ask for help when needed.

Memories that resurface will be difficult after a formal disclosure but is not the same as dribbling and staggering. Any new information you disclose on your own and with the intention to be honest and hold no secrets is admirable. Don't be fooled by thinking there won't be any more questions from your partner. There will always be questions, but not like the number of questions she had for you at disclosure.

Couples that have taken the time to be rigorously honest with themselves and each other by doing the hard work that a formal disclosure requires, can have a new start that inspires hope, a better self, and a stronger relationship. The change that takes place goes deep into the heart of man. Addressing each other's trauma and empathizing takes a relationship to another level, a place that not many couples get to in their relationship. No one else can help your partner heal like you can. You are the one who wounded *and* the one who can help her heal.

When you get to disclosure day, there is relief and a sense of accomplishment: you stayed in the race, did the hard work, and prepared well. A congrats is fitting. Yet, for most men, it does not feel like a compliment. They think, *"This is not what I want to be congratulated on."* I understand, but you endured with perseverance; you stuck through the process and had hope in it, and believed you were doing the right thing. Even when you got knocked down, you got back up again.

I love the story of John Stephen Akhwari, a former marathon runner from Tanzania in the 1968 Summer Olympics. He fell to the ground, cutting his knee open and dislocating it, along with a shoulder wound against the pavement. Most thought he would pull out from the race as he was bloodied and bruised—but he didn't. When asked why he didn't quit, he responded, "My country didn't send me 5,000 miles to run a race but to finish one."[11]

Akhwari was in the race for the long haul. He didn't give up; he didn't look back. He fell and got back up, even though he was bruised and bleeding. He had the tenacity to fight for what he believed in. The work you do for your recovery and her healing is and will be your most challenging run. Even after disclosure, you work as hard as you can to maintain the continuous process of *becoming*. What lies ahead while staying true to yourself and your words and actions is what being a man of integrity is about.

Guidelines for Writing Your Disclosure

The process I've outlined below for writing your disclosure might not be for everyone. Using the words WRITING DISCLOSURE as an acronym gives you a strong starting point and direction as you work through answering some hard questions and detailing some painful scenarios. My hope is that this process will give you clarity as you work toward writing a final and complete disclosure. Much of this will be a repeat of what I've already shared, however, in the following section, we will keep the process all together, *step by step*.

Writing

Writing your disclosure to your partner is much like the first step in Alcoholics Anonymous (AA). However, you are writing the story of your life to your partner and going as far back as childhood. As early as you can remember, write a timeline of events of your life that have led to your recent and present-day behaviors around sexual integrity issues. You want your partner to know the truth as you recall it; you no longer wish to live in secrecy, lying, twisting the truth, and manipulating her reality. You know she needs the truth and deserves it. As difficult as it is to be honest with yourself, it is also difficult for her to hear the truth. A part of her wants all this to go away and pretend like this is not happening, just like it might be for you.

There is relief in allowing the truth to set you free. I hear this all the time. Just think of how long you've been holding this double life and compartmentalizing the hidden parts of you. None of this is easy unless you do the bare minimum. I've had men give me a few paragraphs on a page; this doesn't cut it. Your partner is no fool; she will not accept anything but the truth and all the truth. Like a first step, as you delve into your story, you start to put pieces of your life together. With the practice and patience, you take to uncover and unfold the pieces of your life, you gain an understanding of how you got here to where you are in life.

The fact that you are willing to go through this experience lets her know that you are taking this seriously, you want to help her heal, and you are ready to do what is needed to show her that you are truly repentant, that you want to change from your old ways, and you hope that she will see the new man in recovery that has been brought to redemption. You don't want to rush through writing your story or procrastinate; don't hold back any parts of your story, thinking you've hurt her enough. Many failed polygraphs come out of that madness.

You no longer want to live in secrecy, lying, twisting the truth, and manipulating her reality. Your head and heart know she needs the truth and deserves it, and as difficult as it is to be honest with yourself, it is also difficult for her to hear the truth. A part of her wants all this to go away and pretend like this is not happening, just like it might be for you.

It is essential to come clean and follow the rest of the steps in this process.

Reflect

Reflect on the facts, as you know, and recall them. You are writing to your partner; use her name. Too many disclosures state, *"When you . . . " "she, it."* Instead, address her by name so that she knows that you see her: *"Maria, when I told you I was at my sister's last spring, helping her husband with his car, that was a lie; I stayed longer at the office to watch pornography. I am so sorry, Maria, for manipulating the truth; you don't deserve that."*

Start by jotting down things you know you have hidden from her and a timeline as a rough draft. Be clear and specific as you recall the events, including what was going on in your life then, personally, at work, in your relationship, and what lies you told her. Do not go into blaming or shaming her, as in, *"You were never home, you didn't want sex with me, the children were more important."*

Images

Images of your acting out behaviors may pop up in your mind as you're writing your story and bringing up addictive behaviors.

Don't give the images any thought or brain space to linger. Have a plan, get up, and take a walk. Do not come up with excuses and give them permission to stay around. Talk to the images and voices in your head, like they are separate from you, and tell them they're not welcomed here. There's no room for this in your recovery.

If the images are triggering for you, get on with the plan, take a break, or do something healthy, like call your sponsor or a group member. The images may also be of family of origin wounds, rejection, abandonment, and, worst of all, images of sexual abuse. Do healthy self-care, and return to your writing when you feel stronger and more stabilized. Practicing self-care is not something that most men are familiar with. It comes down to being mindful of your feelings and thoughts and speaking kindly and gently to yourself, as you would want to be communicated to and treated by another, and the way you might reach out to someone who is hurting.

Trauma

According to research, 86% of men and women who have an intimacy disorder have trauma in their lives. Working on your story may activate your trauma. You must be working with someone who is trained and certified as a sexual addiction specialist and understands trauma reactions.

This is one of the reasons you take your time; rushing through this can only make you fearful and ridden with anxiety. When you set yourself up to write your story, hard memories show up: the wounded parts, abandonment, rejection, and even parts that you've put behind you, such as sexual abuse. Self-care is essential; perhaps you have a journal on the side and write about what it was like to have this old or new memory show up, and share this with your therapist.

It's all right to share with your partner that you are struggling with memories; let her know what you are doing about it. It can be reassuring for her to see that you are working through the triggers and not going back to the old coping ways. Staying with the discomfort is new for you; you are going backward to move forward.

Knowing the next right thing to do in a self-care practice takes time and starts with understanding your emotions. Dan Siegel is a child psychiatrist who developed a helpful acronym for helping both children and adults understand their emotions: **SIFT**. It stands for **Sensing**, **Image**, **Feeling**, and **Thoughts**.[12] To work through each letter, ask yourself these questions:

- What are you **sensing** in your body? Is it tightness in your throat, butterflies in your stomach?

- Do you have an **image** in your mind? Is it an abuser, your partner leaving you, crying, or you as a child?

- What **feeling** are you experiencing? Are you scared, angry, sad, happy, excited, tender?

- What are your **thoughts**? Are you wondering if you can get through the disclosure?

Working on your disclosure and being mindful of this acronym in a heightened state of fear and panic can help take the edge off and slow you down.

I as in Self

Statements that start with *I* show that you are being responsible for your actions. Taking ownership for your inappropriate behaviors is vital for your recovery and your partner's healing.

I have heard men say, *"I'm not as bad as some of the other guys in my group. At least I didn't see prostitutes; I just searched for pornography."* I hope by now you know that this is not what I mean here by taking ownership. Instead, taking ownership looks like: *"I looked at pornography and lied about it to you, Julie. I broke your heart and trust in me, and I will do whatever I need to help you heal and trust me again."*

Need

You need to include all lies, secrets, behaviors, and types of behavior. Partners want this information for various reasons—not all, but most. The why and how of their reasons for wanting the information are to be discussed with their therapist.

Knowing and discussing how a particular question might help her process and move forward is essential. Partners already know about a lot of the information they've discovered on their own, what you have told them, and things they have read or heard from other partners. It's hard for them to not ruminate over the images, text, websites they have seen on your devices, as well as information they have gathered on their own. It has severe implications on their minds, bodies, and spirit. They too need counseling to wrap their minds around their new reality. Partners also need to learn ways of coping and healing from the trauma that's been induced.

When she is desperately seeking information before disclosure, remember to practice empathy. Putting yourself in her shoes and speaking lovingly and patiently will soften the reaction. Gently remind her, *"Linda, I know this is important to you, and I am addressing this question in my disclosure; if you have to know before our therapeutic disclosure, help me understand what this means to you, and perhaps we can set up an appointment with the therapist for a pre-disclosure question."* Please don't minimize her or yell at her. Please know that you have a beautiful opportunity to practice empathy, something many of us don't know how to do, but with practice, it gets easier.

Gaslighting

Gaslighting is a term that comes from an old '40s movie, *Gaslight*. In the film, the heroine, played by Ingrid Bergman, inherits her aunt's house and comes to live in it with her new husband, who knows jewels are hidden in the attic. While he's in the attic looking for the jewels, she hears knocking on the walls and all sorts of noises late in the evening. She started to be curious and ask questions. He tells her she's not well, distorting her reality. She also witnesses the gas lights going down at night while he is rummaging for the jewels, and she asks about the lights and he tells her she's imagining things. Throughout the movie, she is made to feel like she is crazy. Slowly, over time, she begins to doubt her sanity and reality. She is made to feel flawed, like something is profoundly wrong and sick about her.

This type of behavior is emotionally abusive. The partners I work with are intelligent women; they come to my office with their facts and research about sex addiction, seeking someone to validate them. They never want to be thrown under the bus again, and never want to be in this vulnerable position again. One of the reasons it's so scary to allow you back into her life is the possibility of it happening again.

Tell her the truth about your actions. Do not gaslight your wife.

Details

Details are a valid source of truth for your partner; it can be a matter of life and death if you have had unprotected sex with other partners. Be sure to include this information with each acting-out person you have been with, including men and women. The dates, with whom, anyone she knows, friends, family, co-workers, neighbors, anyone anonymous, and if you wore protection or not.

Where did you do your acting-out? Was it in your home, restaurants, parks, bars, hotels, or motels? What places have you been to with your acting-out person, and have you been there with your partner? What kind of pornography did you look at, and how and what did it progress to? Did you do drugs or alcohol as part of the ritual? Did you act out in your home, and what part of your home? Did you have more than one sex partner at a time? Did you go to strip clubs? Were you on a business trip, how often, when, where, and what would you report to your partner when she asked out of suspicion or curiosity? Have you received lap dances? What about at massage parlors? What took place? Did you have sex with a masseuse? Did you masturbate? Did you use prostitutes: how often, when, where, any repeats, and how did you find them? Again, what would you tell your partner if she questioned your behaviors? How much money went into this lifestyle? Did you emotionally, physically, or verbally abuse her? Did you have sex with minors? Have you touched any of your children? Are you attracted to the same sex? Has this been your main attraction, have you explored it, and when and how did it start? Did you have unprotected sex?

List the ways you deceived her and what you would say to get her to stop talking or asking about it.

Incest

It's important to include your family of origin experiences with sexual abuse early in the timeline; if this has been a part of your childhood, remember to go at this work slowly, and use self-care to avoid overwhelming yourself. Ask your therapist for help in addressing this major issue and disclosing this trauma, especially if you are just now remembering details. If you have never shared it, you may want a separate session to reveal this part of your life with your partner.

If incest is part of your story, you will need help in identifying and detangling the triggers that show up as a trauma reaction. Differentiating this experience from any other part of your disclosure is important to know how the trauma in your body and mind has impacted you, so you can begin to heal. Helping you make sense of your story is one of the benefits of writing a disclosure. Make sure you're addressing your trauma with your counselor.

This kind of trauma can trigger a relapse, if not handled carefully. Based on past coping mechanisms, amid this hard work, the last thing you want or need is to lose your sobriety and all the hard work you have put into your recovery. If you have been sexually abused, it's never an easy, quick subject to talk about. Address this and get the help you need. You may have to change the date for the disclosure and take some time to work on your trauma.

Secrets

Secret-keeping is destructive. You have led a double life for quite some time. Unhealthy behaviors hijack the brain's development, creating new neural pathways that perpetuate these behaviors and make them difficult to overcome, even when you no longer want them around. Now that you are coming clean and in recovery, your brain is trying to catch up and reprogram new neural pathways. Every new thought you mindfully practice creates a new neuron designed to carry and transmit information to another cell. It is well known that our negative thoughts can drive our anxiety, depression, and aggression, and as much as 80% of our thoughts are a form of negativity. When the old thoughts come around, let them know you are not the same man you were; you are a good person, good-willed, and you no longer listen to the voices that were allowed to deceive you.

Your partner may feel like the secret keeper if you have asked her not to tell. This only adds shame to her trauma. Who you tell and what you say is a delicate issue that will eventually be addressed and agreed upon together in counseling. She needs support, a group, and people she can trust that won't make her feel like she is the crazy one to stay, and hope that you will never hurt her again.

Soon after disclosure, we find a way to tell friends and family why we attend meetings and counseling. But for now, continue to let her know that you brought this into the relationship and plan to work on a way to disclose it to family and friends without her having to hold this information on her own.

Complete

Complete a list of all the secret accounts, email accounts, post office boxes, credit cards, cell phones, numbers, screen names, devices, and the costs. Be willing to take action and let her know how you will go about ending and closing off resources you have used to gain access to your addiction. Whenever possible, delete these accounts in her presence.

List

List all the gifts you purchased for others while acting out and what they cost you. List any items you have received and if you have given your partner any of these gifts you initially bought for someone else. For example, be sure to tell her if there were trips you took with her that were meant to be given to someone else.

Other

Other addictive behaviors: Did drinking/drugging have a part of your acting-out behaviors? How much and how often? The cost? What about gambling? List the amount of money you have gambled away or paid to prostitutes. What about the explicit calls, chat rooms, or websites? How often did you look at explicit images or videos; when and where, and did it go hand in hand with masturbation?

Sex Addiction

Sex addiction has a tolerance level; it can grow out of boredom or curiosity. We want more and more of what that first hit felt like. Where did it lead to, and how did it progress to other behaviors? Did you practice voyeurism? When and where? Did you go to clubs? Did you cross-dress? Were you with prostitutes? Where did you find them? When and for how many hours did you masturbate? Exhibitionism: Where did you expose yourself, how often, and when did this start? Fraternizing: Have you engaged in any of these behaviors: hiring a dominatrix, forcing women to be sexual with you? Any fetish you may have had around sexual behaviors?

Undisclosed

This is your moment. Be honest and do not hold back; your partner does not do well with the trickling of any new information. It sets her back, and any trust that has started to rebuild will be damaged, possibly permanently. For most couples, a polygraph follows within a week of the disclosure. The polygrapher will have questions based on your sexual history and ask if you have intentionally left anything out. You don't want to have an inconclusive or failed polygraph.

Restoration

Restoration is what you want. A restored relationship, redefined, rebuilding after the loss of trust, hurt, relational wounds, betrayal, and rejection. Getting there and giving her what she needs takes time and patience.

I have known partners who ask their spouses to quit their jobs and work elsewhere when the acting-out partner is someone from the workplace. It makes all the sense in the world that you will comply if she is willing to work things out with you.

However long you have been acting out; she will need that same amount of time for healing. Be patient when she's triggered. This is new information for her; you have known about this for months or years. This is why I use the last letter E in DISCLOSURE with the word EMPATHY, and I made an acronym of it, too.

Empathy

You can't do this without the practice of empathy. Empathy is attunement at its best. It is the ability to see, feel, and understand what she is going through. Self compassion goes a long way as well. Be gentle with yourself, feel what comes up for you, and grieve your losses. She sees you as the perpetrator, the betrayer, the rejector; however, you too may have at one time or another been victimized, betrayed, and rejected, and it may help to remember what you needed at the time. It's not easy to hold it all together when you start going through the process. Your partner may not be in a place to help you, nor would she want to while in so much pain herself, but don't ignore your needs. There may be a time when she can and will want to be there for you in your healing process.

An acronym I use to remind clients how to have empathy is this:

- **Empathy**: Put yourself in her place, no judgment.

- **Meaning**: Search for the meaning in her pain. What might be triggering her? You, more than anyone else, can help calm the fear she may be experiencing. Your words and behaviors can assure her that you're sober and safe.

- **Patience**: Put your concerns and insecurities aside while you practice patience and attend to her trauma.

- **Affect**: Get in touch with your feelings, take the time to notice them, and let your feelings speak to your heart. This will allow you to be more aware and authentic with someone else's feelings.

- **Trust**: You will have to earn her trust. Trust takes time to rebuild, time that your addiction stole from you and your partner.

- **Humility**: Humility is a virtue; the opposite is self-absorbed, cocky, and selfish. These traits no longer have room for a man in recovery and wanting to rebuild the trust lost in the relationship.

- **Yoked**: Be equally yoked, serving and carrying each other's burdens develops over a lifetime.

Write Your Restitution Letter

The final part of the disclosure process is writing a restitution letter to your spouse. This letter is read to her one week after the disclosure. This will require serious reflection and consideration of the pain and trauma your partner has experienced. In the next chapter, we will discuss trauma and all the areas and aspects of our lives that it affects, and you will begin to understand how each area of trauma has affected your partner. As I have mentioned, partners want you to know and understand the pain they're in. Having a better understanding of each area of trauma will help you as you begin to process your thoughts and organize them into your restitution letter.

Most men make an honest attempt to be truthful and remorseful; however, it makes sense that there might be several drafts before a final version is reached.

When I'm working with a client, we'll review their draft together, carefully reading through each paragraph and experience. I'll then take time to add comments throughout so that as the client continues working, more of their story can be told and more truths can be disclosed. Tapping into emotions goes a long way—"*I am so sorry you are going through this because of what I've done, you don't deserve this. I don't ever want to hurt you like this again.*"

A client might state that he never told anyone because he stuffed it down, and we'll take that opportunity to explore how and when his addictive behaviors would come up and how to ensure he could be open and honest in the future. Sometimes a client might not remember exactly when or how long the addictive behaviors went on. Those statements are enough to cause distrust with a partner, because of course, how do you not remember something you were involved in? I would council that it sometimes happens that you remember events more clearly as you progress through the healing and recovery process and you could make a note to be truthful and forthcoming as you begin to remember more.

Your brain has been highjacked and as you practice new skills, rigorous honesty, and empathy, you have a better chance of being heard. You can take ownership of your actions and the pain you have caused by stating the exact unwanted behaviors (lying, manipulation, gaslighting, etc.) It is crucial to give a sincere and complete apology, stating why you are sorry and what you are sorry for. Your letter should end with a detailed plan for how you will stay safe, sober, healthy, and honest.

Your partner will also be asked to write a letter for this follow-up session on how the disclosure and discovery has impacted her. She will share any other questions or thoughts she may have on the impact of deception, lies, and gaslighting on her life. What have her thoughts and feelings about your acting-out behaviors been like for her? She is encouraged to write about what the shame and embarrassment have been like. She might share about the damage to her sexuality, her trust issues, the boundaries she would like to set up, and how she will care for herself. What was it like for her to write her impact letter? What was it like for her to hear your disclosure?

I do not recommend that you attempt this on your own. You cannot walk through this process alone. You will need a trusted and safe support system in place: counselor, brotherhood/meetings, advisor, guidance, and sponsor. There are many opinions about what should be included in a disclosure letter. Do your research; ask questions of those who have been through it. Discuss it with your partner, and decide on your own guidelines together. This will give your partner an idea of what to expect. If my outline resonates with you, take it with you to your counselor and discuss it further. Please just remember that it's important to use tools that make sense to you; otherwise, you might not fully invest yourself in the process.

Radical truth is life-changing and the only way to eradicate the lies.

QUESTION FOR YOUR HEART

What might be the most difficult part of writing your disclosure, and how is it challenging for you?

Chapter 3

THE TRAUMA MODEL

> "When they are troubled, we will be able to give them the same comfort God has given us." 2 Corinthians 1:4

In the aftermath of discovering a spouse's sexual secrets and addiction, a partner is traumatized. Most women are blindsided, shocked, and lose their sense of reality. In this chapter, you will learn about the trauma that impacts your partner relationally, emotionally, physically, socially, medically, sexually, spiritually, and as a woman, wife, and mother.

In her book *Your Sexually Addicted Spouse*, Dr. Barbara Steffens, a leading expert on healing from sexual betrayal trauma, writes about how many spouses experience symptoms of Post Traumatic Stress Disorder (PTSD) soon and shortly after discovery.[13] If left untreated, these symptoms can cause significant emotional and physical damage. One of her key findings was that 70% of all partners of sex addicts met all but Criteria A1 (the criteria regarding life-threatening circumstances) for a diagnosis of Post Traumatic Stress Disorder. Some of the emotional signs are anxiety and the inability to stop worrying. Some days, she may feel unattached or have an out-of-body experience; nothing seems to make sense anymore. Her foundation has been stripped to the core, and she can barely hold herself together, which, of course, causes more anxiety and instability.

Life as she knew it has been irrevocably changed. She may not be able to function and manage her life to the same extent she's used to. This only adds to her hopelessness and depression. She experiences sleeplessness and even nightmares. The lack of sleep induces more anxiety and hyper-vigilance, as in racing thoughts, or perhaps hypervigilance, a lack of motivation, and depression. She feels scattered; her thoughts are all over the place. They feel intrusive and unwanted. She is desperate to have the distorted and negative thoughts go away, but her racing mind keeps telling her, *"It's your fault, you weren't good enough, you're to blame for this, this can't be, must be all a dream, how could he do this to me."* Part of her knows the thoughts are lies, yet her thoughts are relentless and persist even at her hardest attempt to stop them from continuing.

To help and support your partner in her healing process, you need to know and understand the trauma she's in. The American Psychological Association defines trauma as "an emotional response to a terrible event like an accident, crime, natural disaster, physical or emotional abuse, neglect, experiencing or witnessing violence, death of a loved one, war, and more. Immediately after the event, shock and denial are typical. Longer term reactions include unpredictable emotions, flashbacks, strained relationships, and even physical symptoms like headaches or nausea."[14]

Dr. Omar Minwalla has developed a model for helping us understand the specific ways that sexual addiction traumatizes partners, called the *Thirteen Dimensions of Sex Addiction-Induced Trauma*. Each dimension is a cluster of common traumatic impacts, traumatic processes, and post-traumatic symptom sequences. He writes, "Not all symptoms may be relevant for every partner or spouse. Trauma is subjective, and individuals are completely different and unique in how they process and express the impact of trauma."[15]

Dr. Omar Minwalla first studied sexual trauma among partners in 2005 and 2006. Dr. Minwalla and The Institute for Sexual Health (ISH) went on to further develop and refine a total of thirteen dimensions of sex addiction-induced trauma among partners and spouses through direct clinical application and grounded-theory research methodology[16].

The Thirteen Dimensions are:

1. Discovery Trauma
2. Disclosure Trauma
3. Reality-Ego Fragmentation
4. Impact on Body and Medical Intersection
5. External Crisis and Destabilization
6. SAIT Hhyper-Vigilance and Re-Experiencing
7. Dynamics of Perpetration, Violation, and Abuse (SAIP)
8. Sexual Trauma
9. Gender Wounds and Gender-Based Trauma (GBT)
10. Relational Trauma and Attachment Injuries
11. Family, Communal, and Social Injuries
12. Treatment-Induced Trauma
13. Existential and Spiritual Trauma

In this chapter, we will explore portions of Dr. Omar Minwalla's *Thirteen Dimensions of Trauma* as we look at several client stories that help illustrate the effects of these areas of trauma. To help you more deeply understand the impact that trauma has had on your partner, you can find more detailed information about Dr. Minwalla's work on the Resources page in the back of this book.

Navigating the Initial Trauma: Discovery and Disclosure

In the onset and much long after discovery and disclosure, a woman loses her sense of guidance and intuition to navigate the direction of her life. She is confused as to what is real and what is not. *"Is this a dream? Will I wake up from this nightmare?"* She can barely make it through each day and hold herself together. Doing the familiar routines and tasks that are required of her as a mother and working woman take every bit of energy she may have. Her ability to make good choices for the benefit of her family is non-existent. She is hardly holding on to herself and needing safety, guidance, help, counseling, and support.

Once the initial discovery is exposed and more incidents are revealed, your partner, will continue to experience and re-experience trauma. The trickling of new information continues to set back her healing experience. Each disclosure is critical and can be a trauma-inducing experience. Going through one disclosure is difficult enough; however, there can be many, including the formal therapeutic disclosure, the trickling in of new information, or an impromptu disclosure that is not organized or planned. Partners can be desperate to know the whole truth and demand that you tell them everything.

Jaime was abused emotionally and sexually as a child, and unfortunately, the emotional and physical scars made it difficult to discern healthy versus unhealthy relationships. Jaime endured far too much in her marriage. She first discovered her husband's indiscretions twenty years into her marriage. Her intuition and awareness of unhealthy boundaries then suffered even more, although she wanted a loving and protective husband and family. She wanted a chance to break through the trauma and evil she had been through with her family of origin. But more betrayals, discoveries, loss of her marriage, and suffering came through the court system as she sought help and protection. *"I started my journey in the court system, a place where I've experienced intense fear, anger, and helplessness,"* she told me.[17] When Jaime discovered her husband's addiction and he finally admitted that he might be an addict, it was agreed he would start therapy. Therapy, however, was short lived and concluded after just two weeks. In her impact letter, Jaime confides that her husband *"unexpectedly hit [her], the last in a long line of increasing abuse from a man who said he loved [her and their] children."* After this incident, Jaime called the police and eventually found the courage to file an order of protection. A step like this takes courage and strength, and it's a necessary step to take when physical abuse is present in the relationship.

Jaime's hope to repair and restore her marriage after discovery ended with the police involved. She never got a therapeutic disclosure. She needed to muster every ounce of courage to move forward and create a new life for the children and herself. She suffered over twenty years suspecting her husband's addiction and infidelities before the big reveal. Finding out about his indiscretions as they continued to trickle in did so much damage to her and the children. Her healing process had to be on hold, while she was trying to make sense of her new reality and do life without the false sense of stability and security, she thought she had. *"How do I take care of and support my children? Where will we live? Can I afford an apartment?"*

One of my clients, Nora, wrote in her impact letter that she had hope to turn their awful situation into something good. The shock she experienced as new information was disclosed made her heart pound so fast, she thought she might throw up. We often don't recognize the physical toll disclosure can have on the body and often clients find it difficult to catch their breath as they navigate the new information being provided to them. Nora noted that the information she was processing was devastating, but that she hoped they could develop a stronger and more intimate relationship. She closes with the words, *"I love you; please take care of my love for you, and don't take it for granted."*[18]

Nora's reaction is an indication of a full-blown trauma reaction, and yet, as she worked so hard to hold onto her faith, she wrote: *"I do believe that God brought us together. I don't think that it is a coincidence that we've been attacked by the enemy, especially with us having a great marriage and other people viewing it that way as well. Satan does not want us to succeed."* Her world had come to a crashing halt after discovering Bill's interaction with pornography and online activity with other women. She felt the attack on her self-esteem; not good enough, not pretty enough, and not sexy enough.

For Bill, disclosure was a relief. *"It was good for me to do that,"* he wrote. *"I released so much stress, and I was able to tell the truth."* He then acknowledged hurt he caused Nora and the fact that now Nora must navigate his betrayal and the lies. In his letter, he states that he is glad to be able to move forward, grateful that Nora is willing to continue the journey of his recovery with him, and ready to start working towards a stronger relationship.

I appreciate that Bill writes, *"I hate what I've done, glad I got caught, I will keep fighting, however, now, you have to deal with all the betrayal and lying I've done."* Bill got it, and yet to what extent did he truly understand her pain? It was important to Nora that Bill hear what she had to say and try to understand the depth of her trauma. *"You cannot begin to imagine what I felt like. I was in complete shock, and my heart was pounding so fast I thought I was going to vomit. I had to keep taking in deep breaths because I felt like I couldn't breathe."*[19]

This couple has been extraordinary in their healing process, and I would attribute it to their faith in God. Since Bill acted out in the workplace, he took great measures to change his environment and schedule. His number one goal to renew their love and trust was in wanting Nora to know her heart was safe with him. Bill wrote his restitution letter without using the thirteen dimensions of trauma, but it was written well and thought out. I have not always used this protocol for the restitution letter. But I am convinced more than ever that the only way to wrap your brain around her experience is to study and reflect on each of these informed approaches to her trauma.

The big scary truth about trauma: there is no such thing as *getting over it or forgetting it*. The five stages of the grief model mark universal stages in learning to accept loss, but the reality is, in fact, much more significant: a major life disruption leaves a new normal in its wake. There is no going back to the old you. You are different now, *full stop*. When your partner is experiencing any hyper-vigilance, hypo-vigilance, mood swings, flashbacks, or other signs of trauma, it's like she's waiting for the other shoe to drop. Trauma is not predictable; it's stored in the memories of every cell in our bodies. Be quick to know this is your opportunity to put on empathy and develop it as a learning moment in helping her heal.

Trauma's Impact on the Mind and Body

The induced trauma and impact on mind and body from sexual integrity issues can have a devastating impact on your spouse's physical body. It can affect both her relationship to her body (how she sees or takes care of her body), cause new medical concerns, and it can alter her personality and who she is inside.

After betrayal, the reality ego is broken and fragmented with the collapse of how she thought she existed and knew herself to be. The reality ego represents who we are, who we become in different circumstances, what we are, what we've made of ourselves, and our self-esteem. Through it we understand and experience ourselves and learn how we interact with others. This ego is part of our personality, and guides what we think of ourselves in any given situation and relationship. What she thought and believed about her world is no longer true. Her life is unrecognizable. In her new reality everything feels disorganized and disoriented.

Minwalla explains, "A traumatized, fragmented, and injured ego causes functional impairment, similar to a brain injury. The ability to utilize the ego towards initiating and effectively implementing health attempts becomes compromised and diminished. The ego seeks repair and integration by attempting to utilize itself to repair and adapt." [20]

The following story is from a woman who believes all treating professionals should know about the functional impairment that is induced when a partner is in a trauma response and still struggling to fully embrace her new reality. Claire is the spouse of a sex addict who was secretly active in his addiction both in childhood and in the first thirty-three years of his marriage.[21] Discovering his secret life was a complete shock for Claire, shattering her world, history, and security. I met Claire at a conference and she shared with me her thoughts on the needs of partners of sex-addicts. She described the difficulties and challenges she faced as she tried to process the traumatic situation she was in, how much of her past was a lie or cover up, and what it would mean for her future.

Claire found it difficult to remember things or navigate day to day tasks. Her brain could not absorb what was happening. She was in crisis, and she found herself distracted by obscure chores like scrubbing the floor and cleaning out the attic, instead of being able to focus on her immediate needs like a shower or meal. She craved sleep and her personality changed as she drifted into survival mode—barely functioning, crying often, and withdrawing. Claire stated, *"My body may not have been dying like a person in medical shock, but my being was. I was entering recovery from an emergency that changed my life and who I am. I needed calming and support."* Claire's needs shifted as if she had suffered significant trauma. During this time, she needed reminders to eat, assistance with preparing meals, help remembering things and events. She also needed safe places to escape to and safe spaces to let her guard down long enough to get real rest. She needed to be able to process her trauma out loud repeatedly, until her brain could rationalize what happened. Claire mentions, *"I needed security and safety. I needed intensive care and was in shock."*

Sometimes a clinical or medical intervention can cause further harm to the victim. Unhelpful and inexperienced treatment personnel can cause a parallel re-injury to the patient or client, including traumatic consequences from clinical interventions, or serious clinical omissions, perpetrated by therapists and medical professionals.[22]

Claire explains that she wasn't just maintaining, but struggling to even just stay afloat, gasping for air while barely able to see a safe place. Claire stresses the importance of pulling the spouse from the depths of trauma and finding the appropriate treatment, help, and support to meet her needs to create an environment in which she can heal. While there may be a time for growth and new skills in the future, the immediate need is to help the spouse stay afloat during the initial aftermath and ongoing disclosures. Claire's story speaks to the experience of many women who have gone through the loss of ego identity and fragmentation, traumatized, injured, and dissolving self. Making sense of our world is crucial to our mental health and stability.

There are many ways the body holds trauma. The partner might develop an eating disorder, whether it's anorexia, bulimia, or overeating; her body is in shock, suffering and trying to manage the new stress. This kind of stress due to her trauma can also cause hair loss, insomnia, crying spells, falling into a fetal position, moaning and screaming for the pain to stop, and not wanting to be touched.

Emily's husband had same-sex attraction, and this affected many aspects of body trauma. Emily wrote that she did all the things she thought a husband would want, initiating intimate moments and wearing clothes she thought he might be attracted to, but that her husband wasn't as responsive as she thought he should have been. She felt like he put up walls and blocked her out.[23] Her body also began to react with physical changes: *"My body started to break down, I gained weight, sleep deprived, I had crying episodes when I couldn't stop, and I had moments when I raged and scared myself. I suddenly was having doctor appointments that led from one condition to another."* When she discovered he was struggling with his sexuality and that it stemmed from childhood abuse, she had a hard time understanding her own feelings on top of needing to navigate what this meant for their relationship. She described to her husband that she felt like he had used her to cover up his homosexual feelings. And despite this, she still *"longed for intimacy with him throughout their whole marriage... Their relationship lacked intimacy in all areas of their marriage, and her body, mind, and spirit needed medical attention."*

The relationship between the mind and body is highly intertwined. Just think of what it was like when you were caught in sexual sin, worried about the outcome in your life and relationships. You might have been sick to your stomach or had anxiety and high blood pressure. The lies we tell ourselves, what we believe as true or not, and how we violated our belief system, lead to bodily stress even when it's exposed and can lead to depression and other symptoms.

Dr. Peter Levine has a beautiful take on how the body holds trauma and how we can be stuck on high or low, and he illustrates that our symptoms are different based on the severity and complexity of the events. A stressful situation for someone who has not experienced trauma can be navigated with a mostly balanced range of emotions, *within a normal range*. If someone has experienced prior trauma in their lives (whether it is physical, sexual, emotional, verbal, or spiritual), new trauma will further complicate and disorient the mind and body connection. At any given time, your partner might enter an overwhelming experience stuck in the high range with rage, panic, and increased heart rate, but quickly move to being stuck in the low range with depression, hopelessness, and fatigue.[24] (To learn more about this and Peter Levine's work, please visit the Resources page in the back of this book.)

Crisis, Destabilization, and Re-experiencing

When we experience external crisis and destabilization suddenly what was familiar and stable in life is thrown into overwhelming chaos. Unexpected change and trauma can make it difficult to get back to normal life in the face of sex addiction. After the betrayal is disclosed, there are a host of logistical considerations that spouses must work through. Are her finances safe? Does she need her own bank account? Will she have enough to take care of herself and her family? Where will she sleep tonight? Where will *you* sleep tonight? Can she take care of the kids? Does she have the stability, or is she too exhausted and sick? Does one of you need to move out? If so, where? How? When? These dynamics are a significant source of stress that alone often causes functional impairment.

If you can't recognize the external and practical stressors that your partner may be encountering—it may look like a sudden shift in living arrangements, childcare, car-pooling, co-parenting routines, what do we tell others and who do we tell, do we get treatment, and at the same time being in a traumatized state—it will only exacerbate her trauma with Sexual Addiction Induced Trauma, (SAIT).

In my workbook, *Spouses of Sex Addicts: Hope for the Journey Workbook*, I include Sally's story. It speaks to the sudden shifts in her lifestyle involving home, childcare, work, what to say to friends and family, and the disconnect between her and the outside world. Sally wrote: *"I began to disconnect from the world. I withdrew from my friends and family. I needed to figure out whom to trust or talk to. I longed to enjoy being with others. Looking back on this period, I don't know how I made it through or how I continued to do the day-to- day tasks at home and work. There were times that I was so disconnected from the world that I would forget to eat, forget to feed my son."*[24] She describes disassociating while grocery shopping or playing with her son—only coming back into the room, into reality when her son begins to say her name repeatedly.

Reactivation and re-experiencing among partners can feel crippling due to the intensity, frequency, and pervasiveness of the unwelcomed triggers. Triggers can be so nuanced and different for every partner, including billboards, magazines, other women, cell phones, blond, brunette or redhead, someone's name, texting, computers, certain cities, massages, intimacy, sexual positions, women of a particular race, and much more. It's only natural that your spouse's defense systems want to protect her. It's painful to ruminate deeply about the things she now knows and wishes she didn't. She's likely to experience panic attacks, anxiety, dissociation, depression, and emotions that are not predictable. Anger can be a coping strategy and a form of dissociation to manage the trauma she is experiencing.

Alice had a calm, patient and gentle spirit, but the pain of trauma and betrayal turned her world upside down. She told me: *"I got so angry that I took our wedding picture and threw it out. Until this day, I am unable to put the picture back up again."*[26] Her ability to function in the real world, as she knew it, is now impaired. Even something as seemingly mundane as checking out at the grocery store now has a different meaning. *"I saw you looking at those girly magazines; you were flirting with that blond woman who was checking us out. The questions seem endless. Who are you texting? What are you doing calling someone at this hour?"* She doesn't want this intrusion to be a part of her life. Much of this type of behavior surprises her more than you.

Everything in her life now feels like a possible source of a threat and further pain and trauma. She may be looking through your phone and bank statements for any discrepancies. She may be looking through your car, trunk, media accounts. She's seeking safety! Her reaction may seem like an overreaction to you, but hear this: it's exhausting; she doesn't want to live like this.

Each story that is shared by the brave women who have been willing and courageous to allow others into her experience has similarities, and yet, is unique to her own life experience and betrayal.

No one intentionally plans to hurt their partners, and you could never have imagined the cost of what discovery would mean and look like for her. I am grateful for these women and their willingness to allow and help you have the insight and understanding in helping your partner heal through their stories. Whether or not you believe this of your partner, your actions make a huge difference in her healing process. Your actions speak louder than words, at least at the onset. Kind and respectful words are always important. Even when you are exhausted, like in the wee hours of the night, and she wants to talk and needs some clarity about something that may have come up that day. Reach down in your heart of hearts and, with kindness and gentleness, answer her lovingly and respectfully. When you can do this, know that you are doing good recovery work and helping her heal. In due time, you can ask for what you need. It's not until one feels heard that one can open up to another's needs.

Triggers are to be expected, and the emotions from a stimulus can be overwhelming. You, too, will experience triggers, whether they are right or wrong. You will be triggered if your partner asks you to leave home for a night or catches you in a lie. Remember, she is trying so hard to hold onto her boundaries, which may or may not have been a common practice. She needs to heal and regain control in her life as she figures out her wants and needs. It may trigger in you rejection, unwantedness, not needed, and negative thoughts about yourself. These are essential feelings and issues to discuss and process in therapy, and at the right time, share with your partner what triggers set you off. In the early stages of healing, she is far from hearing about your needs and wants. Inattentiveness to her wounded heart, dismissiveness, and lack of attunement to what she is going through, will only delay the healing.

Whatever you promise her, keep your word. Don't fall back, don't shrink away, don't cower. You will only hurt yourself and her even more. If she can believe you and know that your word is your word, she will have fewer and fewer moments of panic in the midnight hours.

Sexual Intimacy Trauma, Manipulation, and Gender-Based Trauma

Your struggle with sexual integrity issues can also be a source of sexual trauma for your spouse. The sexual symptoms that a partner experiences often correlate with symptoms of rape trauma syndrome (RTS). "Fear or actual contraction of a sexually transmitted infection or disease is not uncommon for partners."[26] Sometimes, these infections can lead to miscarriage, induced abortions, or other gynecological trauma. The body and reproductive system of a partner may experience numerous physical consequences.

Sexual intimacy is often avoided for various reasons. The challenges a partner experiences might include sexual aversion, avoidance of physical touch altogether, fear of disease, emotional withdrawal, and physical symptoms related to genital and sexual health.[27] Sex Addiction-Induced Perpetration (SAIP) includes different forms of sexual manipulation against partners in an attempt to manage the addiction. These forms of addiction can include marital rape, coerced sex, and might include conspiring with other people who might look the other way or deny the behaviors and manipulation.[28]

Cristy learned about Paul's addiction through several discoveries. At whatever cost, Paul did whatever he could to maintain and manage his addiction to pornography and masturbation.[29] He was caught time after time, but continued to manipulate Cristy to have his way and lie to try and hide his addiction until Cristy no longer felt safe with him. She realized she couldn't stay and finally created a firm boundary: she would no longer live like this. In her impact letter, she states: "When I found out that you had chosen to deceive me, it changed me and my response to you."

Cristy goes on to explain that each time she was betrayed or lied to, she questioned the person she knew her husband to be. She could no longer trust him as her partner, and he was constantly making it clear that he only cared about himself. The question is no longer "is it true?" but now, the question is "what else are you hiding?" When you discover your marriage has been full of lies and hidden secrets, it's difficult to undo the damage and rebuild that trust. *"Each time you took a step to maintain your secrets, I took a step to protect myself from your addiction."*

Tamara wrote about the impact on her sexuality after finding out about Ian's same-sex attraction. She felt as though she was not enough, that something was wrong with her, and the lack of intimacy made her think she had to prove herself as a sexual being, as well as living with the fear that Ian was not faithful to her. [30]

For most of her married life, she experienced *sexual shut down*, and not knowing the secrets Ian held, she went into protective mode with fear and anxiety of contracting a sexually transmitted infection or disease. Tamara married Ian, their intimate life was comfortable for a while, and then she became disappointed. There was something preventing closeness and pulling them apart. Ian told her there was something wrong with her, but Tamara began to understand the truth—it wasn't her. Her desire for sex went away after her hysterectomy: *"I learned to channel my needs in other ways, not sexually."* And Ian only desired intimacy with her if he used pornography, which further reduced any desire she might have had to begin with. Tamara began to see how Ian reacted to men when they were in public, and she soon realized he had no desire for women, only men. *"I did not realize that he was fantasizing about his encounters with men to keep an erection."* As they began therapy to rebuild and restore their marriage, Tamara felt she had to prove herself to be desirable. A 90-day abstinence period was suggested and only added to her confusion. Tamara explains that the impact of his addiction on her emotional and intimate needs, and how she felt that sex was the only way to have a happy and normal marriage.

Discovering a spouse's betrayal and sexual addiction damages these core pieces of identity, including your partner's identity as a wife, mother, female, and sexual being. Gender identity and gender esteem are a primary and core dynamic in the development of our sense of self, our core self-esteem, and our self-worth. It can destroy your partner's sense of worth and her body image. But the impact of gender wounding on overall psychological health and functioning is often not recognized.

Lori wrote her impact letter to Jim one week after their formal disclosure. So many things were now starting to make sense to her after years of living like she did not matter and feeling like she only existed to serve Jim's needs.[31] As a woman, she felt diminished and used for the many sacrifices she had made to be the perfect wife that she believed she should be for Jim. She wrote to Jim:

BECOMING

> *"My heart aches and is filled with great sadness for me and my self-esteem. The traumatic injuries that you incurred to me as a woman, your wife, and mother of your children, my sexuality, and spirituality have all been impacted by your irresponsible dominant self-seeking behavior, as I was made to feel less than when all I wanted was for you to be happy."*

Lori was relieved to discover Jim's infidelity at first, because it provided proof that she wasn't crazy. But then the pain she felt swallowed her and she wanted to disappear. She felt worthless, humiliated, betrayed and worthless. Jim controlled every aspect of their household, the family budget, and even her life. *"I compare my life to one of those movies where the women are kidnapped or deceived and somehow bribed to live in a cult, where the abuser, manipulator, fills her up with false doctrines, deep down in her heart she knows something is off, and yet under those conditions she stays."* She lost her sense of self and the lines between right and wrong began to blur.

Lori began to pinch pennies to be a good steward and stretch their income. She always put the children's needs before her own, but always bought new clothes for Ian. And there were times when there wasn't enough food in the house. In her impact letter remembers, *"I never told you; I did not want you to worry. You robbed me of your time, time that should have been invested in me, and our family. You robbed me of your tenderness and love that belonged to us, but you preferred to give it to your prostitutes . . . Let's not forget my cooking, cleaning, laundry, taking care of the children, and working twelve-hour days. You used me to be the trophy wife so you could continue hiding and protecting your secrets."*

Gender wounding puts a woman at risk of falling short of who she is, being untrue to herself, and inevitably questioning her self-worth and intuition. Lori is not alone; her story speaks to many women's experiences. Her belief system has been shredded and violated, and she concludes that she is not good enough. She has been used, and her needs as a woman are not important; she exists to make him look good. Lori says, *"I wish that you had a little compassion for me and took me seriously. My body is alive, but you have killed everything inside of me. I came to the conclusion that you found pleasure in humiliating me and seeing me suffer, without any remorse, as you did this time after time. I get horrified thinking that for over thirty years, I lived with a man that just wanted to use me for material benefits."*

How Addiction Trauma Affects Other Relationships

The impact of addiction trauma can be felt in each layer of your partner's community; inner, middle, and outer circles feel the ripple effect of the trauma. The inner circle includes the relationships closest to her heart, like family and close friends she's in contact with on a regular and daily basis. These people have her heart and trust. Her middle circle of community includes on-going relationships with neighbors, church friends, extended family, and others with whom she interacts frequently. The outer circle may be acquaintances, social media friends, and people she has known over time, but not folks that she connects with either on an emotional level or even that often. Whichever circle they are in, she may be isolating and avoiding herself from them for various reasons.

Healthy and secure attachments to human beings are essential to psychological health. Relational trauma and attachment injuries, including attachment rupturing and traumatic relational dysregulation within the system of the relationship is another critical injury of sexual addiction induced trauma.[31]

Riley writes with the hope of wanting restoration in the aftermath of discovery and disclosure and is still shaken through and through. Sexual addiction induces a traumatic rupture in a relational attachment.[32] What Riley believed to be a healthy and secure relationship was now anxious and insecure in the shake-up of her confidence. She believed they had a strong faith and bond as a family, and a lasting, loving relationship that would endure all things. Over time, Riley found her way back to the confidence and security she had known about herself, was able to ask for what she needed from her partner Sam, and find her way back to herself. She wanted to feel safe and secure in her marriage, set boundaries and limits, and give herself time to understand the changes needed for Sam to work a healthy recovery program. Riley writes, *"I definitely have hope that trust can be restored, but my confidence is shaken, and we have had multiple relapses over this last decade. I know that my hope remains in Sam's relationship with our Lord, genuinely pressing into him instead of just trying to do the right things."* Riley begins to realize that she must take better care of herself, instead of catering to Sam's need, or even making herself available to the kids. She needs to hold herself to being his accountability partner, instead of stepping in to pick up his slack. There's a shift in their relationship that needs to happen, and it starts with shifting her priorities to caring for herself first.

Often, partners of individuals struggling with sexual integrity "end up holding secrets from loved ones and family," and adding strain to other relationships in their lives. Trauma might also make them pull away from community, avoiding social interactions, and change the way they interact with others or their faith. This trauma not only affects the partner's inner world, but it also alters the way connections are formed, disrupts trust and dependency with outside communities, and it's "common for many of these often extremely painful dynamics to go unacknowledged and excluded from discussions on sex addiction."[33]

Most couples with a family have many concerns and questions about how and what to tell their children, regardless of age. Some choose not to say anything to them about the sexual integrity issues. Often, it's the partner of the acting-out person who prefers to keep silent. She may feel this way because of shame, or the desire to protect him from any awkward social encounters. She may not want her children to feel bad about themselves or their father because of the indiscretion, or she may fear what they might think of her for staying. Sometimes it is necessary to tell the truth or say something, particularly if jail time or treatment is a factor. What does she say to people in the circles of her life? It's not easy, no matter the situation or outcome. Disclosing to family members and friends is a decision you make with your partner, deciding how much or little to tell.

If you decide to tell your story to family or friends, then you should be the one to disclose it, *not her*. One way to do this is to write a letter and state how you are responsible for the pain she is in. They will have an opportunity for questions at the end. Write your letter in age-appropriate language. Set up a time and date with your loved ones and let them know you have a very important letter to read to them. It's important to disclose to your children and whomever else she may want you to.

Mark read this letter to his adult children after we reviewed it together several times: *"This letter is to help me stay focused, as I tell you the truth of the sinful acts I have done, and what has been happening over the last fourteen years, as well as before I married your mother, and more importantly the last seven to ten years."*[34] Mark outlines for his children when he and his wife started marriage counseling in 2004 and explains that even then their mother only knew a small part of his secrets. *"I was a shadow of the person you thought your father was. I had hidden secrets that no one knew, and I kept them to myself."* Mark admits to being a fraud and not upholding his duties as a father, husband and a Christian man. He spent many years trying to remain in control, and ultimately, disclosing his sexual integrity issues was the only way for Mark to regain control and begin to rebuild the relationships that mean the most to him. *"I knew I did not want to go back to the lowest spot in my life. I had to be completely honest for the first time in my life. She was traumatized by the truth. This truth-telling has caused your mother trauma and has questioned everything over the last 32-plus years, I take full responsibility."* In his letter, Mark discloses to his children that he is in recovery for sexual integrity issues, that he has struggled with pornography since he was ten years old, and he also committed adultery in his marriage to their mom. Mark owns the hurt and trauma he has caused their mom and his children—noting that he recognizes that he cannot be a good father to his daughters when he treats other women as objects for his pleasure. Mark is willing to do the hard work of *becoming*, surrendering himself to God, and committing to individual counseling, couple's counseling, and attending a men's group frequently.

Over the years, Mark has had a radical change of heart; his family has noticed the process of his *becoming*. They now have a real relationship, and he's taken off the masks he once wore as a cover-up. They have mutual love and respect. Mark went on in his letter to address each of his children, ask forgiveness, and speak about the moments he was unavailable to each one. I especially liked what he wrote to his son warning him that pornography will ruin his ability to truly feel emotions: *"I truly have not been a true man for you. A lot of talk, but surely not enough actions to show you or talk to you about protecting yourself from getting caught up in the garbage I have. I truly pray that you do not live in your father's sins."*

Our actions significantly impact others, especially our families. They count on us and lean on us to be role models who take responsibility for teaching what is good, pure, and righteous.

A young woman told me a story about her dad's indiscretions. She stated that as they were out on a walk together, she noticed her dad's wandering eyes and how he did nothing to look away from checking out women he was attracted to. He was clueless as to how that impacted her as a daughter and woman. Her parents divorced because of her dad's sexual integrity issues. She felt shame as if it were hers to hold. She stated,

"I gained an understanding of what it might feel like to be a partner of someone with sexual integrity issues, something I wasn't looking for."[35] Her dad could not move away from the lust of the eyes, protect his daughter's heart, or hold himself accountable for his actions, and she suffered because of it.

When Her Heart and Soul Need Rescuing

Time and time again, we ask ourselves, *"Where is God in my pain?"* It makes sense that a sexual integrity issue would feel like a spiritual rupture. A spiritual relationship with our Creator is sacred. It's the most important relationship we can have. In our quiet moments, we may not feel God's presence. The voices in our head begin to ask, *"Where are you God? Why are you allowing this in my life?"* There were times at the beginning of the discovery process that I had a hard time drawing near to God. I felt shame, wondering how this could have happened to me. Wasn't I a good person, a good enough wife? *"God, where are you? Why would you allow me to suffer like this?"* I called on friends who had no idea what was happening between my husband and I, and I would ask them to pray for me. I knew they didn't have to know what it was about; they would be my prayer warriors. I would ask that they specifically pray that I would continue to believe and feel His presence and that He would give me strength and courage for the day.

I asked and prayed: *"This is too hard, God. Why, Lord, just why would he lie and keep secrets from me and think he could get away with this? How does he think I can stay in a relationship with him and ever trust him again? You knew all along, God—why did you allow this? Why didn't you stop this? Why did this go on for so long? Why didn't he get caught sooner? How did I not see this coming?"* I am so thankful we have a patient God who knows our hearts and loves us no matter what. He knew the outcome. He knew one day I would be writing to you and be able to say, I am grateful that God has transformed both our hearts, and we have a God that heals our brokenness. It all matters to Him.

However, in the process of becoming healed, I would question God's existence in my life, and in some ways, this felt like a spiritual crisis. I knew in my heart that God would never leave me or forsake me. The transformation that took place in my heart was a life-changing journey. I learned how deeply God wanted me to heal and how I needed to allow Him in His timing to reveal what He wanted from me. I needed to get out of His way while he worked on my husband and not try to be the Holy Spirit. I learned that I needed to always seek God's ways and His purpose for my life, no matter what lies ahead. He wanted my heart, soul, and mind to surrender and trust Him. John Ortberg experienced the Dark Night of the Soul and when God was silent, he called Dallas Willard. Dallas responded, "This will test your joyful confidence in God. Isn't that painfully beautiful?"[36]

Thankfully, my faith and ability to trust God is even greater now than before, and I have the strength to see the beauty in the *testing of our joyful confidence* that God has done in both of our lives. Only God could have been so tender with my heart to get me to a place of trust and submit to His will, while working on trusting my husband once again. I knew I didn't want a divorce and break up our family, and I eventually started to see that my healing process had made me stronger emotionally and spiritually. I am grateful that my husband allowed God to cut away at the impurities that blocked his heavenly view of the God he now knows as his Lord and Savior. As for me, it developed a strong spiritual backbone in me that led me to believe that I could be used to help couples work their way through the trauma and recovery work that my husband and I have been through. I became a certified sex addiction specialist and worked on a program with Barbara Steffens, creating a trauma model for professionals who treat partners.

This chapter on trauma is heavy with a lot of difficult personal stories. I hope you take the time to reflect on each area of trauma and consider its impact on your partner. Please understand this is not presented to shame you, but to give you a better understanding of what your partner is experiencing in the aftermath of sexual integrity issues. In her mind, she struggles in every way to move on, get her life back as she knew it, and not have to fight the images, thoughts, and feelings that haunt her.

Many of my partner clients have stated that they aren't honest about what they're going through because their partner goes to shame, and then they feel like the perpetrator. They admit that their partner doesn't understand the number of triggers that appear everywhere and anywhere and at any time, which can be tiresome and exhausting. They're told that they should be over this by now, and that begins their own shame spiral and struggle.

Keep in mind that she doesn't want you to have cause for further shame; in fact, she desperately wants you to get better and experience a life without shame hovering over you. In the next chapter, we'll talk more about why recovery and shame can go hand in hand and why it is crucial to separate the two.

QUESTION FOR THE HEART

After learning more about the different areas of trauma and their impact on your partner, what is your takeaway?

Chapter 4

YOUR BRAIN ON SHAME AND OTHER EMOTIONS

"I prayed to the Lord, and he answered me. He freed me from all my fears. Those who look to him for help will be radiant with joy; no shadow of shame will darken their faces." Psalm 34:4-5

Shame is how addictions survive.

Shame has no limits or boundaries. It affects us all, men and women, regardless of who we are, or what we do. Left untouched, it will align itself with a fundamental feeling of being flawed. It becomes the fuel that drives the engine of negative behaviors.

In the *New York Times* bestselling book *Healing the Shame That Binds You,* John Bradshaw writes, "I used to drink to solve the problems caused by drinking. The more I drank to relieve my shame-based loneliness and hurt, the more I felt ashamed. Shame is the motivator behind our toxic behaviors: the compulsion, codependency, addiction, and drive to super-achieve that breaks down the family and destroys personal lives. It limits the development of self-esteem, causes anxiety and depression, and limits our ability to be connected in relationships."[37]

Your brain on shame is precisely where the addiction wants you to be. Shame will convince you that you are a bad person and leave you in a state of worthlessness. It will have its way with you and repeat the cycle of addiction, telling you that you will never change, that you're not good enough, that you're defective and flawed. When shame is speaking louder than hope, you may not have the fight to defeat it, and you will begin truly believing the lies that say you are not good enough and not even God would forgive you. In that state of mind, shame makes you feel invisible and of no value to yourself and others.

Understanding the Brain on Shame

Our brain reacts to shame as a threat, shutting down parts of our nervous system. It threatens to activate the frontal lobes that control our executive functioning because it feels like we are in imminent danger. These vital organs monitor and organize our thoughts and feelings, preventing them from going to the outfield and functioning on all gears. Our frontal lobes manage impulse control and problem-solving skills, expressive language, and memory. A continuous and repetitive flow of shame recycling in our brains changes our neural pathways, damaging brain tissue and impairing our frontal lobes' best performance and functioning.

Deep within the limbic system of our brain is the amygdala, which is highly useful in detecting threats and danger. This is the brain's fight, flight, or freeze center. The amygdala is also responsible for processing and regulating emotions. This tiny part of our brains can shrink or enlarge with chronic stress, depression, anxiety, and shame can contribute to either of these conditions. While your brain is detecting and encoding a shameful experience or memory, you get thrown into a pattern of either fight, flight, or freeze, and your frontal cortex goes offline while the amygdala, the center of your emotions, takes over.

If your amygdala is detecting fear and danger, it is ready to get to work on your behalf. Unless you recognize the incoming threat that says danger, and slow yourself down, shame, fear, and other emotions will take over. The amygdala is doing its work, whether its fight, flight or freeze. However, it also disables your ability to be fully present and functioning.

There are a few basic skills you can use to help calm your amygdala's response. Use the six-second breathing technique to slow you down.

CHAPTER 4: YOUR BRAIN ON SHAME AND OTHER EMOTIONS

Take a deep breath in for six seconds, and breathe out the toxic shame for six seconds. Cortisol is a hormone in our bodies that is essential in maintaining blood pressure, immune, and anti-inflammatory functions. Under stress, which is often caused by shame, our cortisol levels increase, putting us at greater risk of diseases, including diabetes.

Taking vitamins and Omega-3 fatty acids (brain food), and going for walks (moving your body) can alter your brain for the better. Having and using all checks and balances in your recovery protocol promotes a healthier limbic system and a calmer you.

I love Dr. Daniel Siegel's works on interpersonal neurobiology, a field that helps us understand the mind and mental health. Dr. Siegel's hand model of the brain structure is a great way to help us visualize how our brain functions.[38]

Look at your hand and imagine that your brain resembles a closed fist with your thumb (the limbic system—the "big emotions" of your brain) tucked safely underneath your fingers (the prefrontal cortex—the rational and thinking part of your brain)—the brain can connect with all its parts on board, sending signals and messages that can be decoded.

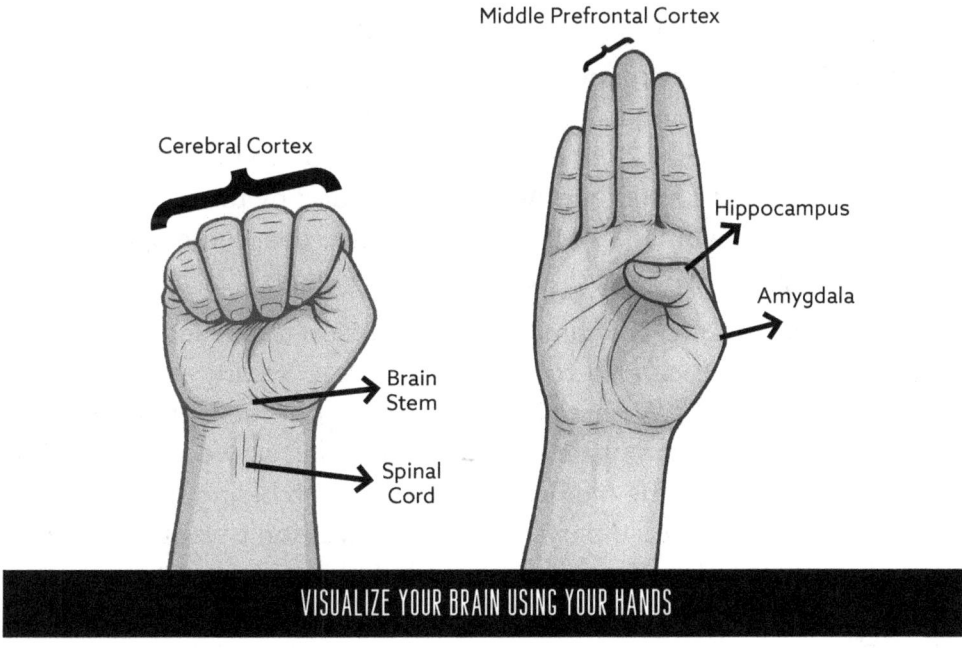

VISUALIZE YOUR BRAIN USING YOUR HANDS

When we're under stress, our brain reacts (*pull your fingers up and away from your thumb*), limiting activity in the prefrontal cortex. Siegel refers to this as the *flipped lid*. Our brains are considered to be *offline* and the connection is lost. Our body and minds sense a threat. We lose the ability to think constructively and positively, and instead, we operate from a place of high emotion. This reaction from the limbic system is your brain screaming danger since you temporarily do not have full access to your rational and thinking prefrontal cortex.

Shame can take over, and you lose your full potential to connect to the highly functional, rational, thinking brain. In that state, you are unable to give your very best to your partner. And of course, a disagreement or heated conversation never goes well when both of you have a *flipped lid*.

How does your shame, shame you? Do you shut down, freeze, fight, or flee? What is your pattern? Know how to restore a fully engaged self, one that can be clear, concrete, and concise in difficult moments, or when triggered. If nothing else, breathe in and out, nice and slowly.

The Effects of Shame

Shame also makes us want to hide. Genesis 3:8 tells us: "The man and his wife heard the LORD God walking about in the garden. So they hid from the LORD God among the trees." How did Adam and Eve know to hide? God had given them clear and specific instructions: "You may freely eat the fruit of every tree in the garden--except the tree of the knowledge of good and evil" (Genesis 2:15). Adam and Eve stood to fail as they manipulated and shamed each other. Adam blamed God by telling him that he had given him the woman. "At that moment their eyes were opened, and they suddenly felt shame at their nakedness" (Genesis 3:7).

In his book *The Soul of Shame*, Curt Thompson discusses what hiding and holding secrets can do to our inner being: "Hiding is the natural response to shame."[39] We hide from ourselves, our feelings, values and principles in every imaginable way we run as far as we can get away with. Furthermore, all the hiding we do starts with hiding from our own selves. There are multiple parts of self that we don't want to know. It would be too shaming. This might include judging, lying, stealing, gluttonous, hoarding, lusting, adulterous, and arrogant selves, just to name a few. But as David Benner points out, quoting John Calvin, "We cannot expect to know God fully if we are not willing to know ourselves, for one depends on the other."[40]

Shame is a vulnerable feeling and scary to expose. Sadly, perhaps, as a child, you told yourself or were told messages like, *"I'm not good enough, I will never be as smart as my brother, you should be ashamed of yourself, you're naughty, you'll never amount to anything, you're just a silly little crybaby."* We are most vulnerable to this type of toxic shame as children. It creates feelings of embarrassment and inadequacy. It only takes hearing these messages over and over in different settings of your life to become the toxic shame. Take the time to notice what it is like for you and what happens when you feel humiliated, defensive, fearful of being judged or rejected. What is your knee-jerk reaction? Do you want to hide, run, collapse, apologize, get defensive, or run to addictive behaviors that you use to escape? I challenge you to slow down and be curious about the strong emotion that bombards you. These emotions may be trying to protect you from the overwhelm of shame. When fear or any other feeling is threatening to shut you down, use your skills that keep your brain intact, like SOS, because fear can be emotionally crippling when the hippocampus brings up a stored memory of a specific event you have experienced.

One way to better understand ourselves and our shame is through parts work, a theory called Internal Family Systems, or IFS. Richard Schwartz is the founder of this unique modality.[41] In IFS, Schwartz teaches that parts of us are there to protect us in some way—even the parts of ourselves that seem self-sabotaging. Your inner critic is a part of you trying to protect you in one way or another; it may sound like this: *"Don't even try; you know you're going to fail."* The critic doesn't want you to fail, so why even try. If we don't take the time to listen to some of the voices in our head, we lose out on an opportunity for growth and freedom from hiding in shame.

According to Schwartz, our parts have three primary categories: Exiles, Managers, and Firefighters. Exiles are the younger parts of self that hold emotions, vulnerabilities, needs, and memories that went ignored, unresolved, and went into *exile*. Managers are the parts that keep *going and doing*. They help put the exiles aside so that the functioning part of the self can go on with life. Managers can be healthy or unhealthy. The ability to suspend and put things on hold for the right time is a good self-managerial skill, but putting constant stressors on yourself to avoid your emotions or being a perfectionist is a manager part of not wanting to deal with reality.

A manager may even show up as anger. Firefighters are extreme versions of *managers*; they act more impulsively and are desperate to make any emotional pain go away. They might present with addictive behaviors, shutting down (dissociating and disconnecting from self and others) or self-destructive behaviors. The intent is to keep the younger wounded parts exiled. Firefighters are fearful of what will emerge if exiles return.

Your exiled and wounded little self needs the wise you to stay integrated. We do this by checking in with ourselves, making sure brain parts are working together, talking to each other, and keeping shame from hijacking your brain.

Think of it this way: it's like you have a village of little exile parts, managers of all ages in different stages of your life, as well as firefighters that show up in addiction, shopping, eating, drugs/alcohol, perfectionism—you name it. They're all a part of this little village that lives inside you. You can talk to them anytime. The shame part loves to be the first to remind you; *"I can't believe you did that again; you said you were going to stop; didn't you say you would never do that again? You're such a failure; you'll never change."* But a healthy question to ask yourself is, *"Whose voice is this? Could it be the voice of a caretaker in your life? How old is this part that is showing up?"* Know that part and be familiar with it; you might call it the critic or the judge but know it well because it can destroy you if you allow it to have its way with you. Speak to it, and let that part of your brain know it's taking up too much space in your head, and that you have no tolerance for this abusive talk. You're done with those shameful messages. Give your wise-self permission to take over.

Some parts, like the dissociative parts, believe they are protecting you. A painful memory is triggered, and the dissociative part is right there to keep you from feeling the shame and emotional pain of a particular memory. Jack, for example, was shamed as a child when he cried at the loss of his childhood pet. *"Only sissies cry,"* his dad told him, *"Toughen up and be a man."* A few years later, when his grandpa died, he noticed his dad never shed a tear.

When I first met my client Joseph, he understood that he could no longer live in the shame of his past failures. He longed to break free from the clutches of shame that held him in bondage to a pornography addiction he had many years before and into his marriage. After many years of meetings and mentoring other men, he longed to enjoy his marital relationship, be free of shame, and experience the joy and freedom of forgiveness and working a healthy recovery program. [42] He wrote in his disclosure, *"Our marriage and our lives have been on pause for way too long. You mentioned that we have been living individual lives on two different planes. We've lived from various perspectives that are currently not complementary nor bringing us closer together but conversely creating an ever-growing rift between us. The time has come when we must decide to move forward together as a united couple or move forward and go our separate ways."* Joseph acknowledges their vows of better or worse, richer or poorer, in sickness and in health and affirms his commitment to their marriage stating, *"Too much pain, bitterness, and anger have been present for way too long in our marriage. These all need to stop."* Joseph pleads with his wife to replace all the pain and hurt with unconditional love, support, and acceptance. And later in his letter, he tells his wife that he will do what it takes to battle sin and temptations for the rest of his life so that he becomes a better man and husband. He tells her that *"together, they can achieve their dreams and can continue to help others as God presents opportunities."* Joseph knows the first step to moving forward together is acceptance: *"This doesn't mean forgetting the past but starting each new day, believing in each other, fighting for each other, and working together to make our dreams come true."*

Joseph is a good man and wants his marriage to work. He does not want any part of shame that controls his ability to love his wife or himself. He admits he still struggles with "lust hits" and understands that his ongoing participation in program work is needed and beneficial to maintain his recovery and sobriety. He has worked hard at combating the negative thoughts, beliefs, and images he has of himself for bringing pornography into his life and relationship. He longs for the marital relationship to be healed, to belong and to be cherished by the woman he loves.

The History of Your Emotions

Few of us grew up in homes where we were encouraged to feel and sit in our emotions, explore how they show up, and talk about them. It's important for us to understand where some of our feelings and thoughts originate.

Before we could express ourselves in words, as infants and toddlers, we spoke the language of feelings and could experience ranges of emotions from happiness and joy to fear, sadness, and anger. Studies tell us that children in orphanages who are not touched and cared for by loving caregivers grow up avoiding touch and are fearful and unaware of their own feelings. Their experience in these formative years goes on to affect their emotional, physical, and mental development throughout their life. While you may not have been born in an orphanage, perhaps your emotional development was delayed because of trauma or addiction. Traumatic events, as well as addictive substances, can stunt natural emotional development and derail the limbic system that is responsible for processing our emotions. Some of us are acting and responding out of immature, underdeveloped brains.

To better understand your emotions and your own philosophy behind them, in his book *What Makes Love Last?*, John Gottman walks you through a series of questions for several different emotions—encouraging you to dig deep and be honest with yourself about the way certain emotions show up in your life.[43] Gottman encourages you to feel your way through your feelings and hang out with them to become familiar with them, as these provocative questions stimulate feelings that we sometimes want to avoid. Feelings are what they are, and yet we don't need to act on all of them. Try practicing radical acceptance—it does not mean we have to like or approve of our emotions, but the key is not to judge our feelings. Addressing these basic feelings and learning more about how you maneuvered and managed your life through some painful life experiences will give you a greater insight into some unwanted behaviors. (Please visit the Resources page at the end of the book for more information regarding John Gottman's work.)

Jack learned at a young age that feelings were not safe to express. He couldn't be authentic with his feelings without shame reminding him, *"only sissies cry, so buck up."* The internal voices of criticism and shame became loud enough that his "managers" could no longer hold back, and his *firefighters* came to his rescue. One day, he found his dad's pornography stash in the bottom of a dresser drawer while hunting for a jackknife. At eleven, he had never seen anything of this sort. His curiosity got the best of him. He hid one under his shirt while ensuring the rest remained in place. Jack would get lost in the hours of combing through the magazine, losing track of himself and time. He eventually got good at trading one magazine for another in his dad's drawer and spending more and more time in a world of fantasy.[43] This world kept the feelings and thoughts from crossing over and reminding him of how worthless he felt.

Change Your Beliefs, Change Your Feelings

Understanding feelings is half the battle. What you tell yourself when a specific event or action takes place will affect the outcome and experience you feel as well as how you move through the situation. Albert Ellis is the founding psychologist that developed Rational Emotive Behavior. He viewed our negative thoughts as coming from our irrational beliefs about ourselves and others. In his book *A Guide to Rational Living*, he states that, "people often 'awfulize' or 'catastrophize' turning small setbacks into unbearable disasters in their minds."[44] He created the ABC model illustrating how events filter through our belief systems to impact our feelings.

The actual event activates the belief system, and the belief system stimulates the consequential feeling of believing the messages you're telling yourself about the event. For example, you may come home from work and find your front door locked, and after trying to unlock it a few times, it still doesn't open. This is the *Actual Event* in Ellis's model.

Then we have the *Belief System* that kicks in and says: *"She changed the locks, I knew this would happen, she's going to leave me, I'm not worth staying around for, I'm not trying hard enough, I'll never be good enough."*

Then we have the *Consequential Feelings*. Thinking and believing the messages you are telling yourself are followed by consequential feelings of fear, shame, anger, or sadness. It all traces back to the belief system. What we tell ourselves and believe about it makes a big difference in how we react (or not) to the activating event.

We have something like 12,000 to 60,000 thoughts in one day.[48] Will you allow negative thinking to take over? Or will you replace the negative thought with a healthy, realistic, positive thought?

I've been known to expand this model to include the additional letters D and E to remind us to *change* the beliefs that result in our negative thoughts and feelings.

- ✎ Dispute the Belief System: *"How do I know she changed the lock? It could be just a coincidence."*

- ✎ Exchange the negative thinking: *"I am good enough; I am working hard to repair and work on myself and relationships."*

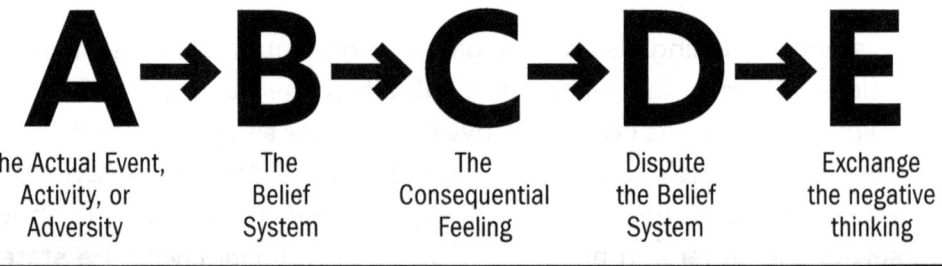

ABCDE MODEL, ADAPTED FROM ALBERT ELLIS' MODEL

What we allow to run through our brains is highly influential. Pay attention to what your thoughts are and what you say to yourself. Have boundaries over what you allow others to say to you, and monitor what you watch, and listen to. Our brains retain the information we put in it. Also remember your thoughts may originate from specific messages you took on as a child. Practice discernment and allow your wise self to be in charge, rather than the negative, abusive, shaming voices from the past. Dispute the negative messages and replace them with positive thoughts. Know that with every new thought, our brains form new connections and neurons, what scientists call neuroplasticity in the brain.

QUESTION FOR YOUR HEART

How does shame challenge you, and what obstacles get in the way of shame having its way?

Chapter 5

WORKING A TWELVE-STEP PROGRAM

"The LORD is my shepherd; I have all that I need. He lets me rest in green meadows, he leads me beside peaceful streams. He renews my strength. He guides me along right paths, bringing honor to his name." Psalm 23:1-3

Bill Wilson suffered from alcoholism and was hospitalized several times for the treatment of alcoholism before he reached the age of 39. While lying in a hospital bed, Wilson wrote about his depression and spiritual awakening. "My depression deepened unbearably and finally it seemed to me as though I were at the bottom of the pit." He still had bits of doubt and denial about the presence of a greater Power, and as he surrendered his pride and stubbornness, he cried out: *"If there is a God, let Him show Himself! I am ready to do anything, anything!'* He goes on to describe the room lighting up "with a great white light" and a wind of Spirit, not air, blowing at him, eventually the feeling of elation faded away and he found himself still in the hospital bed, however, transformed. His writing continued as he described *"a wonderful feeling of Presence"* that surrounded him and went through him and then he says: "*I thought to myself, 'So this is the God of the preachers!' A great peace stole over me, and I thought, 'No matter how wrong things seem to be, they are still all right. Things are all right with God and His world.'*"[46]

A "Higher Power" is something greater than ourselves. It's a term used in Alcoholics Anonymous (AA), founded in 1935 by Bill Wilson and Dr. Bob Smith. Wilson found his higher power to be God and even in moments of despair and doubt, he saw God show up in ways that couldn't be missed. Your Higher Power will become a crucial piece of recovery, especially in a program such as AA.

AA was inspired by another Christian organization called the Oxford Group, which was founded in 1921. Frank Buchman, Lutheran minister and the founder of the Oxford Group, believed that surrendering one's life to God was the only way to peace and reconciliation of our wrong-doings. He emphasized a relationship with Jesus Christ rather than any works we could do to merit salvation. The Oxford Group believed in four absolutes taken from scripture, and these four virtues were also carried over into the AA program several years later by Bill Wilson.

1. **Love**: 1 Corinthians 13:4-7

    "Love is patient and kind. Love is not jealous or boastful or proud or rude. It does not demand its way. It is not irritable, and it keeps no record of being wronged. It does not rejoice about injustice but rejoices whenever the truth wins out. Love never gives up, never loses faith, is always hopeful, and endures through every circumstance."

2. **Purity**: Psalm 51:10

    "Create in me a clean heart, O God. Renew a loyal spirit within me."

3. **Honesty**: Proverbs 10:9

    "People with integrity walk safely, but those who follow crooked paths will be exposed."

4. **Unselfishness**: Galatians 5:24

    "Those who belong to Christ Jesus have nailed the passions and desires of their sinful nature to his cross and crucified them there."

If you've ever felt like you've hit rock bottom, you know it's a painful process; it's a feeling of deteriorating from the self you knew, while experiencing hopelessness and disparity. Rock bottom can take you to a point of feeling like there's no return. It wouldn't take much to convince you that things couldn't get any worse, although they sometimes do. While I hope you never get to that point, it is often necessary to do the healing recovery work available in twelve-step programs.

Many other twelve-step models, such as Narcotics Anonymous (NA), Gambler's Anonymous (GA), and Sex Addiction (SA), are offshoots of AA. But no matter who we are and whatever journey we are on, we can all adhere to and live by the twelve steps. I love the idea of using the steps as a personal mission statement. They give us direction, keep us honest, and help us to own up to our weaknesses and failures. We work on our defects of character while humbly making amends. I like to think of the twelve steps as a refining process: "Remove the impurities from silver, and the sterling will be ready for the silversmith" (Proverbs 25:4).

The Twelve Steps of Alcoholics Anonymous:

1. We admitted we were powerless over alcohol and that our lives had become unmanageable.

2. Came to believe that a Power greater than ourselves could restore us to sanity.

3. Made a decision to turn our will and our lives over to the care of God as we understood Him.

4. Made a searching and fearless moral inventory of ourselves.

5. Admitted to God, to ourselves, and to another human being the exact nature of our wrongs.

6. Were entirely ready to have God remove all these defects of character.

7. Humbly asked Him to remove our shortcomings.

8. Made a list of all persons we had harmed and became willing to make amends to them all.

9. Made direct amends to such people wherever possible, except when to do so would injure them or others.

10. Continued to take personal inventory and when we were wrong promptly admitted it.

11. Sought through prayer and meditation to improve our conscious contact with God as we understood Him, praying only for knowledge of His will for us and the power to carry that out.

12. Having had a spiritual awakening as the result of these Steps, we tried to carry this message to alcoholics and to practice these principles in all our affairs.[47]

We are all in a continuous flux, always learning and constantly changing. Step ten tells us to do an ongoing self-assessment and own up to our offenses. It is not natural to catch those wrong doings immediately. We must practice and be intentional. The twelve steps are a lifetime practice of learning and relearning through our mistakes. David the psalmist prayed for an undivided heart, one that would transform his heartened heart. "Teach me your ways, O LORD, that I might live according to your truth! Grant me purity of heart, so that I might honor you" (Psalm 86:11).

Recovery and twelve-step work is demanding and exhausting. Meetings are there for teaching, community, and accountability. Finding the right sponsor can be a challenge; he must himself have addressed and worked through step two which ensures he has found a Power greater than ourselves and believes that Power can restore us. He must also have a good record of staying sober and not be timid about calling you out to the twelve steps of recovery. He must understand how denial, deflection, manipulation, and lying are destructive to your sobriety. You want a sponsor who keeps your feet to the fire while encouraging your faith in God. It's a high calling, and yet the men I know that are sponsors gladly take this role on and give back what was given to them. Step twelve is an example of men and women who have experienced success and want to help others—they are called to carry the message of healing to others and to practice the twelve steps throughout their lives.

Your faith will give you the strength to unwrap the unwanted behaviors and tentacles that have choked their way around your heart and mind. You are no longer held captive to the lies and lures of what addiction promises to deliver. My question to you is, *"Have you surrendered to God as your higher power? If not, what are the obstacles and challenges that get in the* way?" God is the final authority on our lives and where we spend eternity. He is the one who knows our hearts and wants salvation for us more than anyone else. If you believe in the word of God, you can experience and know that He gives understanding, spiritual wisdom, and the ability to trust and know Him better. If this is true of you, you're on the right track! If you're unsure, I assure you that God won't let you down. He delivers what He promises. If there's ever a time in your life when you need Him, it's now. He wants to rescue his children from the harm and evil that the world can inflict on us. He wants to give you a peace that surpasses all understanding.

Making Amends

Each of the twelve steps has a set of principles and values to work through. They are all for your benefit, and no one else wants this more than you. If you have not made it a practice to study and work on the twelve steps, I highly recommend it. It can take weeks and even years to get through all twelve. For our purpose of healing from sexual integrity issues, I'll be addressing step eight because it's crucial for understanding and repairing with your partner.

Step eight in the AA model tells us to make amends as part of the healing and recovery process. One of my clients, James, wrote a list of his losses and regrets, which helped him to recognize the damage that had incurred from his infidelities. This list was simply a starting point to help him navigate as he began his journey of *becoming*:

"What I have lost:

- Eva's trust . . . Eva's trust . . . Eva's trust . . .
- The look of what Eva sees when she looks at me
- Eva's joy
- The special relationship between Eva and I
- The look of love in Eva's eyes
- My self-respect
- Potentially lost health of myself and Eva's due to HPV

- Being able to see and spend time with friends
- The ability to say that Eva was the only person I had been with
- Years of my life that I cannot take back

What I regret:
- Not coming home to Eva in the beginning
- Listening to the bad advice in my head from my "lust brain."
- Spending the money that we could have used elsewhere
- The cold-hearted things I told Eva in the beginning
- Not telling Eva everything upfront rather than dragging it out for five weeks
- Causing Eva to have her mind flooded with images she should never have seen
- Having to pretend that everything is good when we're around our children
- All the pain I've caused Eva
- Yelling at Eva, not really because of her but because of my guilt, shame, anger and frustration
- Spending too much time, energy, and money on prostitutes

What I have gained: *a relationship with God, a surrendered heart that no longer needs to control everything, peace beyond understanding, Eva can now look at me and know that I am being truthful."*[48]

James knew and understood it would take years to repair Eva's broken and traumatized heart. He knew that over and over he would need to make amends and rebuild the trust he had forsaken in their marriage.

In his book, *Worthy of Her Trust,* Jason Martinkus provides a wonderful tool to guide you in writing an amends letter to your partner/wife, called the Amends Matrix.[49] The Amends Matrix is a great tool for a thorough apology; nothing that is needed to be said is left undone. There is no room to mess up an amendment with Martinkus's matrix. The matrix starts with listing past offenses that are showing up in the present with similar

CHAPTER 5: WORKING A TWELVE-STEP PROGRAM

patterns of what took place in the past, and helping you understand the effect of your actions and feelings. The questions allow you to investigate both your behaviors and your feelings about them, and allow room for you to include how you feel about your partner's feelings. Finally, you will conclude your amends with how you want the issue at hand to be handled in the future and how you would like your partner to experience the changes you will implement.

Most times, saying "sorry" just isn't enough. *What exactly are you sorry for?* By using this model and following the steps to write out your sincere apology, you will fully understand what you are apologizing for and how to truly work towards amends. Remember, you may think you're 100% right and she is 100% wrong. But coming from a place of true repentance, respecting her point of view, and protecting her heart from any future pain will ensure a better result.

This is my recommended process for navigating amends with your partner, and this guided amends exercise is an excellent tool to have in your tool bag. It's helpful to clear up any misunderstandings, guide a thorough apology, and even deal with unresolved issues from the past.

A Guide to Making Amends

The Amends Matrix

Step 1: What's happening now that connects to pass pain or disappointment? Trace the touch point.

Remember that your past is now her present. As more and more of your past behaviors are disclosed it causes strong reactions and emotional distress in the present.

A key step in a thorough apology is creating a safe space where your partner can share her pain while connecting the current trigger to something that is linked to pass pain and tracing it to the here and now situation. This involves reflecting on your past actions and how they continue to affect your relationship in the present. Recognizing any specific actions, thoughts and feelings you may have had about a situation or behavior from the past, such as your partner asking if she could look at your phone. Previously, you might've blown up and told her she had no right to go through your phone. All the while hiding secrets you kept from her that might've been discovered if she went through your phone. By acknowledging how the past is now influencing your present behavior of being secretive, you're demonstrating that you're working towards transparency and responsibility in owning any behaviors that may resemble an out-of-control reaction to her inquiries towards your recovery process.

Step 2: What exactly happened in the past? Tap into the past.

This step fosters transparency, without deflecting, denying, or minimizing. It shows your partner that you are willing to make a sincere apology and develop restoration. It is critical that you are clear and honest in disclosing specific actions that have perpetrated and violated her trust. This kind of transparency and vulnerability helps your partner to know that you understand her pain. Any kind of past behavior that is reminiscent of your acting out, stunts her ability to heal. You are far better off to take the time to sit in the past and recognize the patterns of your behaviors originate.

To continue the example about the phone in Step 1, you might've lied to her and told her you left your phone at work. Think about how lying showed up in your life, where did you learn this, how did it come about. In Step 2 you would admit that you lied about leaving your phone at work when you feared she would find your email for escort services. In admitting how her distrust around phone issues and lying to her makes total sense as to how it may retraumatize her, and as painful as it is for her to hear, you are validating her new reality.

Step 3: Why did you behave this way in the past? Find the why behind the what.

This step involves knowing yourself to help your partner heal. You are uncovering the underlying issues of your harmful actions, and this requires an understanding of the root causes that drove your behaviors. You may have been seeking escapism from unresolved trauma, acting out due to past wounds, seeking validation, engaging in addicted and compulsive behaviors as a way of escaping the pain in your own life.

Following through with Step 1 and Step 2, you may uncover deeper truths about some of your own behaviors that distracted you from being honest with yourself. Telling lies as a kid and getting away with it, is one thing, embellishing the truth, and others thinking it's cute, is another thing, but as adults carrying an encyclopedia of lies in its worst scenario can be chronic, and even pathological.

Taking responsibility for your own actions and choices, and avoiding blaming others is a way of showing how the *why* in your life has a past and how it's relevant now in rebuilding trust and a new future. This step not only helps you understand the destructive patterns in your past, but it also helps your partner process pain she may be inflicted with, and a better understanding of issues in your life.

Step 4: How do you think she must have felt? Be present in her pain.

In this step, you are shifting from your apology to putting yourself in her shoes. By validating her emotional experience, you are demonstrating the ability to be trusted. You are moving beyond self-focused from the shame and guilt to tuning in to her feelings.

Using the acronym SAASS (scared, angry, anxious, sad, shame) might be beneficial in understanding where she is coming from. As you write Step 4, ask yourself, *how might she have been scared that I would not allow her to look at my phone? Did she have a right to be angry about it, how would I react to that? Could this have caused her to be anxious and compulsive about looking at my phone? Knowing what she now knows about my lying I can only imagine how sad and depressed she must be.*

The shame and humiliation you experienced from discovery/disclosure, is now running through her veins. She doesn't want to carry this. What you think and say to her carries a lot of weight. Each step of the amends matrix is meant to slow you down and think about the ongoing impact your past behaviors have led to. The effort shows you are trying to understand and prioritize her feelings.

Step 5: How does it make you feel, knowing that she felt this way? Engage empathy.

As you move thoughtfully through each step-without rushing to offer her just anything-by the time you reach Step 5, you'll find your self-awareness has deepened. Step 5 invites you to engage with your emotions to understand the depth of her trauma as a response to understanding her pain.

Not only are you giving her a thorough apology, but you are also practicing empathy. Attunement is an emotional resonance that aligns with the feelings of another. It's a deep connection that responds to your partners emotional state. At its very best, you are suspending any judgements or criticism, and into the heart of a shared experience mirroring their feelings. Take my acronym for EMPATHY with you along in writing this step.

Step 6: How do you want her to feel now?

Step 6 builds on the previous step. You need to demonstrate that you are well invested in her healing processes. Let her know how important it is to you that she feels safe, that you are protecting her heart, and that you truly want to change and be the trustworthy man that she deserves.

What you were and did in the past is not you anymore. You, more than anyone else, do not want the unwanted behaviors to rear their ugly head again. Let her know that you cherish her, you want her to experience peace from all the pain and anxiety of past lies. Let her know what your desire and actions are to make things right for her feel secure. All of this takes time, as you well know. It does not clear up in one amends letter. You are expressing a need for her peace of mind and happiness. Articulating these positive intentions can make a difference in her healing process.

Step 7: What do you want the future to be like? Cast the vision.

In Step 7, you are letting her know that your thoughts for the future are thoughtfully expressed with a vision that ensures her emotional safety around the issue at hand. She does not have to experience anxiety around lies and the phone issue from the past. Let her know your desire for her is that she will trust you and believe you are being truthful. Tell her that you want her to know that the change of heart in you is to deepen the trust, respect and commitment to her ongoing healing process.

Your commitment to your recovery work from the lies and secrets is for transparency and open access to any of your devices. Cast the vision that you are working towards a future built on radical honesty and openness, where she never has to feel the past pain of the anxiety that comes from wondering if you are being truthful or not. Let her know you want her to feel confident and secure in moving forward together. Give her permission to ask for an amends matrix anytime she is feeling the need for reassurance.

Take your time, take a breath and pray. If your feeling overwhelmed, judgmental, angry that you have been asked to write this up, you need PRAY (pray, read God's word, ask for what you need, yearn for what is good and pure).

Martinkus's Amends Matrix is a great model for putting your thoughts down, staying on track, and giving a thorough and clean apology. And I hope my guidance through each step helps explain the process a bit more and allows you to fully understand what an amends process should look like. Writing it out helps slow down our brains and reactivity; we're better able to focus and be clear-minded. It also allows you to write about the issue without interruption and fear of rejection or shutting down from emotions ramping out of control. In conflict, our knee-jerk reaction isn't normally to respond with empathy and to speak clearly about the offense; we typically get defensive. You may shut down emotionally, and that can appear as you don't care, or cause you to say things you regret. Let your partner know that you want to make a rightful apology/amends. Inform her about the Amends Matrix. Please give her a timeframe; the sooner you make amends in the aftermath of a rupture, the better it will turn out. Invite her to ask for a written amendment whenever she needs one.

Here is an example of what Bob wrote to Emily in his disclosure and amends letter. He combined his amends at the end of his disclosure, using all seven steps to express what was on his heart. Bob connected the past and the present, why he responded the way he did, acknowledging what he's done to change while offering empathy to her situation, stating what she must have felt, how he understands what it must be like for her, and casting a vision and expressing hope for the future.[50] *"I honestly don't know how possible or difficult that may be, but I sincerely hope that, with continued help from counseling, I can reverse the trends of the past and lead you to feel a depth of love and warmth for me as your husband that you have never thought in the first part of our marriage."* Bob continues to write that he wants his wife to feel loved and wants to be her protector and best friend. He affirms his commitment to recovery and that he hopes for their home to a safe place for her and all their family. Bob is hopeful that they can restore their relationship and their remaining years will be full of joy and love. He writes that he understands her reaction to his behaviors and that he will continue this journey of healing and recovery with patience, honoring her timeline and ensuring that she is comfortable throughout the process. Rebuilding trust and healing a broken heart take time. It's important to not rush the process, to hold space for reactions and emotions that might be hard to hear.

> *"I do love you, my dear Emily. Thank you so much for graciously giving me a chance to prove it. It is a gift that I know I do not deserve, but I am so very grateful you have been willing to give me this chance.*
>
> *With all my love, Bob."*

His letter was beautifully thought out and well stated. Bob and Emily are among the many successes in this journey of recovery and healing. It takes rigorous honesty and a commitment to *becoming* and waiting with expectations, as we'll discuss in Chapter 7. Bob writes in another part of his disclosure of the hard work he's done and says, *"I do acknowledge and understand your skepticism and anxiety about ever trusting your heart to me again or being willing to be vulnerable with me. I do acknowledge that I must always work to prove myself trustworthy and to provide a place in our home and in my heart where you will feel loved, protected, and cherished as my wife."* Bob has worked an extensive amends process, and he is full of hope for the future with his spouse. He expects to be truthful with himself and Emily in the process of renewing his heart and mind, as he *"always works to prove himself trustworthy."* He wants Emily to feel *"loved, protected, and cherished."* He could not have expressed his true self without surrendering to God and spending time in prayer that their remaining years would be full of joy, love, encouragement and hope.

The Brotherhood

> *"Let us not become weary in doing good, for at the proper time we will reap a harvest if we do not give up."* Galatians 6:9 NIV

You need the brotherhood to lift you, hold you in prayer, and give you words of encouragement. They know what it feels like, they've been there. Step eleven of AA says, "Sought through prayer and meditation to improve our conscious contact with God as we understand Him, praying only for knowledge of His will for us and the power to carry that out."

Don't go into a victim stance; stay strong and be courageous. In the beginning stages of discovery and disclosure, you are building stamina and endurance. It will feel rocky for both of you, like learning a new culture or language. You will feel alone, but you're not. The brotherhood may be a new concept to you. We are not meant to do life alone; we need each other. You learn from each other; you sit eyeball to eyeball, hold each other up in prayer and pray for your brothers' recovery work to be the best it can be. We are to love one another as Christ loves, and that means when you see a brother down, needing encouragement, be there and help lift him up.

"Be careful then, dear brothers and sisters. Make sure your own hearts are not evil and unbelieving, turning you away from the living God. You must warn each other daily, while it is still 'today' so that none of you will be deceived by sin and hardened against God. For if we are faithful to the end, trusting God just as firmly as when we first believed, we will share in all that belongs to Christ. Remember what it says: 'Today, when you hear his voice, don't harden your hearts as Israel did when they rebelled'" (Hebrews 3:12-15). Remember, you're not beyond temptation, and you're never alone. Your higher power, God, is with you; he will not leave or forsake you. "When troubles of any kind come your way, consider it an opportunity for great joy. For you know when your faith is tested, your endurance has a chance to grow. So let it grow, for when your endurance is fully developed, you will be perfect and complete, needing nothing. If you need wisdom, ask our generous God and he will give it to you. He will not rebuke you for asking. But when you ask Him, be sure that your faith is in God alone" (James 1:2-6).

I cannot say it any better than the scriptures: take heed, brothers, men who want to do the right thing, who want to save themselves from the condemnation of guilt and judgment know that your higher power, Jesus, has paid the price. "Therefore there is now no condemnation for those who are in Christ Jesus, because through Christ Jesus the law of the spirit who gives life has set you free from the law of sin and death" (Romans 8:1-2 NIV). Please make meeting with an accountability person a priority.

Below are some questions you can bring to the table and use with your accountability person/sponsor. It's best to meet at least once a week.

1. Have you been respectful, understanding, and kind with your words and deeds this week?

2. Have you been truthful and honest with your feelings and thoughts this week?

3. Have you given in to any lustful thoughts and addictive behaviors this week?

4. Have you done your twelve-step work or any assignments given to you this week?

5. Have you honored boundaries that have been set up between you and another this week?

6. Have you held any grudges, resentments or anger toward anyone this week, and what have you done about it?

7. Have you needed to make any repairs/amends with anyone this week, if so, why or why not?

8. Have you taken the time this week to spend with your higher power? What are you getting from your readings, and how is it impacting your life?

9. What challenges and obstacles did you encounter this week?

10. How will you be safe, sober, healthy and honest this week?

11. Have you been completely honest with me?

QUESTION FOR THE HEART

How often do you turn towards your higher power? Why and why not?

Chapter 6

HELPING YOU HEAL

> "So get rid of all the filth and evil in your lives, and humbly accept the word God has planted in your hearts, for it has the power to save your souls . . . But don't just listen to God's word. You must do what it says. Otherwise, you are only fooling yourselves. For if you listen to the word and don't obey, it is like glancing at yourself in a mirror. You see yourself, walk away, and forget what you look like. But if you keep looking carefully into the perfect law that sets you free and if you do what it says and don't forget what you heard, then God will bless you for doing it."
>
> James 1:21-25

In this chapter, we will look deeper into the root causes of some of your behaviors to help with understanding and healing, and we'll explore some helpful tools and exercises as we dig deeper into recovery.

We all have childhood wounds. Unless you've done your work and addressed these painful events, they show up in unexpected ways, including chronic diseases and psychological disorders. Wounds can manifest as trauma and can lead to the use of mood-altering drugs, addictions, escapism, sleeping, over-working, perfectionism, and eating disorders, among other things. Exposing these wounds helps you to understand these negative behaviors. It can also strengthen your emotional intelligence, impulses, and self-control. You can make connections from the past to the present and uncover secrets that have been compartmentalized or avoided.

Looking in the mirror is not an easy thing to do when all we see is our imperfections. We see things most people don't. We hear voices in our head that remind us of how flawed and imperfect we are. If this is what you see and hear about yourself, there's a good chance that there are some childhood wounds. We all have secrets and things we have kept to ourselves.

Healing starts to take place when we reach deep down inside of ourselves and allow the memories to come up and sit with them as long as we can endure, without going into the trauma vortex. The trauma vortex will suck you into a web of emotions that are out of control. And most likely, most of us don't know our way out unless you're shown or told how to manage the overwhelming feelings. Help from a therapist is recommended as you begin to work through events that have a traumatic impact.

One of my clients, Eric, experienced trauma in his childhood which became the point of origin for sexual addiction in his adult life. His struggle with sexual integrity had a direct negative impact on his relationship with his partner. Eric's childhood trauma affected his ability to engage in healthy relationships with others while hindering his understanding of appropriate interactions. He acknowledges the impact his behaviors had on his relationship and how it interfered with their closeness, never allowing them to fully engage in intimacy: *"My eyes and heart were blinded. I now know that because of my past behavior, you may never fully trust me, and that is a cost I am reminded of each day."*[51]

If Eric had not taken the time to know and understand himself, he may not have been able to begin to heal himself and save his marriage. There are many benefits to looking into our souls for healing, purging the lies we've told ourselves, making amends with those whom we've hurt, and learning how to forgive those who wounded our own hearts, mind and bodies.

Compartmentalizing may have been the route you chose to keep you from experiencing the pain of your abuse. Statistically, around 80 percent of men and women who struggle with sexual integrity issues were physically and emotionally abused, and more than 80 percent say that they were sexually abused.[52] The wounded parts of you that have been abandoned beg for your attention. It takes faith and courage to trust that God, in this process, will give you the bravery you need to take one step, one moment, and one day at a time. "When your faith is tested, your endurance has a chance to grow. So let it grow, for when your endurance is fully developed, you will be perfect and complete, needing nothing" (James 1:2-4). Your healing means an opportunity for growth and enlarging your capacity to "get rid of all the filth and evil in your lives, and humbly accept the word God has planted in your hearts, for it has the power to save your souls" (James 1:21).

I appreciate how Peter Scazzero states the importance of addressing our past, and going back to move forward. Sitting in some of your deepest losses and pain can help you discover how courageous you are. He states that the "gravitational pull back to the sinful, destructive patterns of our family of origin and culture is enormous. A few of us live as if we were paying for the mistakes of our past. For this reason, God has called us to make this journey with companions in the faith. Going back to go forward is something we must do in the context of a community with mature friends, a spiritual mentor, a director, a counselor, or a therapist. We need trusted people in our lives to whom we can ask, how do you experience me? Please tell me about your feelings and thoughts when you are with me. Please be honest with me. Prayerfully listening to their answers will go a long way toward healing and getting perspective on areas of our lives that must be addressed. This takes a lot of courage. This work of going back to go forward certainly leads most of us to the Wall in our journey with Christ. We find ourselves disoriented, confused, and shaken by the unknown territory to which this leads."[53]

It's time to consider writing a personal mission statement, as well as a couple's mission statement. This can be grounding and stabilizing before you start the trauma work. It gives you a sense of who you are and where you hope to go in life, while working through some of your very difficult life stressors and events. *Remember: You are not the trauma, but the trauma did happen to you.* I have previously mentioned that the twelve steps of AA would be a great mission statement and example to work from. By writing your mission statement, you are reminded of your values and principles. It keeps you anchored in the present and offers hope for the future. Your mission statement also serves as strong boundaries, keeping you accountable to your on-going recovery, avoiding self-doubting or catastrophic thoughts of your past experiences. Here are some ideas of what you might include in your mission statement:

1. I seek God first in all my ways.
2. I seek to be a man of integrity and trustworthiness.
3. I practice self-care and seek to have balance in all my doings.
4. I seek ways to love myself, and my family and am committed to being a caring, compassionate, and loving man.
5. I have weaknesses and strengths that keep me humble and serving others.
6. I am a good man.

The following example of James and Eva's mission statement is an agreement in keeping to priorities for the sake of their relationship. They use their mission statement to keep each other accountable and honest. For example, they might use statement four to say, *"I'm not feeling supported."* Since their mission statement speaks to their relationship requirements, it becomes a gentle reminder to turn things around, connect with a positive outlook, and have a conversation that needs to happen.

1. Smile! With our mouths, eyes, and heart
2. Show affection to each other
3. Be respectful of the other's needs
4. Be supportive of the other's feelings
5. Communicate with an open mind and be willing to hear another perspective.
6. Feed the spirit with daily devotions
7. Share your feelings openly through the lens of love, if we are not able to, ask for a timeout and reflect on what God might have for us to learn.
8. Share thoughts and ideas in the spirit of love
9. Listen actively
10. Honor commitments

11. Make Christ the heart of our relationship, body, soul, and spirit

12. Total honesty in all things, including sobriety

It takes a lot of effort and consistency to unlearn some of the bad habits we've developed. We need to be steadfast, jump-in and roll up our sleeves to do whatever it takes to practice and take on the new.

Looking Back to Move Forward

An important part of recovery is to look back into your childhood and pull painful memories to the surface so that you can begin to process what happened to you, when it happened to you, and how those experiences guided your life up until this point. Your body has held on to trauma, whether you are aware or not, and as you begin to process where you came from and how you go to this place, it will be important that you rely on supervision and support as you release negative energy and traumatic events you may not have processed. Therapy won't take the memories away, but it can help you to understand the story behind the wounded parts of you. When you're doing the work of looking back to move forward from some of your most challenging and painful memories, it opens your heart and mind toward the truth and healing from the past. As you unleash the powerful hold these memories have had on you, the truth will break through and set you free from the grip it's had on you.

When you're actively working through trauma, I suggest slowing your pace—stopping every twenty minutes or so to evaluate your level of distress and overwhelm. The following adaptation of the SOS model is a simple and easy tool to use as a check-in while doing this kind of intensive work.

- **Stop**: Stop and check in with yourself; while doing this work, you want to be able to self-regulate and think clearly. A pulse oximeter is a good instrument to have on hand for heart rate. If you're in distress and your heart rate is anything over 100, you're not regulated. It's time to take a time out, slow down and take some deep breaths.

- **Orient:** Orient to the here and now. Feel your feet on the floor, back against the cushion, and hips on the chair and be curious about anything that comes up. Pay attention to what you notice as you check in with what your body is experiencing. Use your senses to stay present: touch, smell, taste, hear, and sight; this is especially helpful if you tend to mentally wander.

- ✏️ **Scale:** Bringing up something you have compartmentalized in a "do not disturb" area of your brain will be distressful. You will want to ask yourself, on a scale of 1–10 (ten being your worst experience, and one is a positive experience) about each experience. Notice if anything is coming up, like a knot in your gut, an image, a feeling, or perhaps an awareness. Slow yourself down, take a deep breath, and ask yourself what needs to happen now to lower your distress level. What do I need to do to have control of my feelings and thoughts? Calling a friend or counselor may be necessary before you continue working through your trauma. You may also think about setting up an appointment with your counselor before you continue the work.

It's important to connect the patterns of your life, learn how to process the big traumas (Big T's) and the little traumas (Little T's), and understand the effects the trauma has had on your life. There's an incredibly useful tool to help you work through this called the Trauma Egg, originally created by Marilyn Murray as part of her theoretical treatment model for emotional trauma, and then later adapted by Patrick Carnes for treating sex addiction. Working through this exercise can be difficult and I highly suggest you consider doing this with the assistance of your counselor. [54] If you have already done one, do it again. You might be surprised to find that it looks a whole lot different now that you're in a different stage of life.

To work through the Trauma Egg exercise, you will write your family mission statement. What stands out from your childhood? Perhaps something like, "In my family of origin we did not air our dirty laundry." From there, you'll fill in the roles your family members had—who was the responsible one, the scapegoat, or the family hero? What other roles were represented? Then work your way to the family rules (spoken or unspoken)—"In our family, we had to be perfect" or "In our family we couldn't talk back or express an opinion."

CHAPTER 6: HELPING YOU HEAL

FAMILY ROLES

....
....
....
....
....

FAMILY BOUNDARIES

....
....
....
....
....

FAMILY RULES

....
....
....
....
....

TRAUMA EGG

DAD

....
....
....
....
....

MOM

....
....
....
....
....

Next, we'll look at characteristics of your parents. Was it your experience that your mom presented herself as a "nurturer"? Did your father present himself as an "angry man"? With each characteristic write a few details about how you experienced each parent in those roles, before the age of twelve.

Here are several questions to consider as you progress through the Trauma Egg exercise: How have these roles and characteristics carried into your adult life? What patterns do you notice that are familiar to your family of origin and repeated in your adult life? Do you see that you behave in similar ways as your parents? How so? In the center of the egg, you will create bubbles and fill those in with a drawing of an experience. If you're not artistic, this can feel like a challenge, but never fear, there are no grades for this assignment! You can also consider filling in the bubbles with words that have a meaning to you and it will still be effective. The idea is to start in the lower section of the egg with your earliest memory of stressful and trauma events that took place in your life, and move up towards the top of the egg through the present time.

Take your time to slow yourself down. Pause to notice and acknowledge the feelings you may be having as you do the work. Are you able to make sense of those feelings without becoming overwhelmed? It can be a tricky task, but it's important to go slow, take breaks as needed, and use your tools and support systems. This is not something you will complete in one sitting.

EMDR, *Eye Movement, Desensitization, and Reprocessing* can be incredibly beneficial as you recall trauma and you begin healing by reaching into the past to move forward. With a protocol for a safe place in mind, you focus on an event utilizing bilateral stimulation with a light bar. Consider a young child experiencing a trauma event—they're most likely not able to make sense of what is happening but can only remember feeling scared. If they were told "not to tell," this trauma is held in their body until they face it one day in the future—either unintentionally through stress behaviors or with the intent to heal from it. Reprocessing an experience through EMDR allows your adult mind to integrate and release these traumas. A few things can come up—feelings, meaning, or sensations—as you reprocess the experience. There are therapists that are specifically trained and certified to do this work. Don't try this on your own, as it takes experience to walk someone through this process. The goal is to bring the subjective unit of distress to a lower level, if a triggering event comes up, and sometimes a new and relevant meaning is experienced in a new and different way about the situation.

When you begin to unravel and process, even reprocess, experiences from your past in a safe environment, you begin to have clarity about your life circumstances and you can begin to regain control of situations you once thought were hopeless.

Avoiding a Relapse

You are not alone in your temptations. Remember 1 Corinthians 10:11-13: "If you think you are standing strong, be careful not to fall. The temptations in your life are no different from what others experience. And God is faithful. He will not allow the temptation to be more than you can stand. When you are tempted, he will show you a way out so that you can endure."

I think of Joseph as one of the great patriarchs of the Old Testament. The Bible tells us he was a handsome and well-built young man. The king of Egypt, Potiphar, realized that the Lord was with Joseph in all his successes, and Potiphar found favor with him. He put Joseph in charge of his entire household and trusted him with all his business affairs. Potiphar's wife desired Joseph and wanted to sleep with him, but Joseph refused.

Joseph responded, "My master trusted me with everything in his entire household. No one here has more authority than I do! He has held nothing back from me except you, because you are his wife. How could I ever do such a wicked thing? It would be a great sin against God" (Genesis 39:8-9). Potiphar's wife continued to pressure Joseph, but Joseph remained strong and steadfast against her temptation. Eventually, Joseph had to physically tear away from her advances. As he ran from the house, he left his cloak behind in her hand (Genesis 39:10-12). Wow! What courage, strength, loyalty, spirituality, conviction, and endurance!

Best of all, I love that he tore away and ran from evil. If anything shows up like this—an unsavory ad pops up in an email, a former lover or prostitute contacts you—follow Joseph's example and run the other way. Unfortunately for Joseph, it did not end well. Potiphar believed his wife's lies and many privileges were taken from Joseph—a price he paid for doing the right thing. And if you know the rest of the story, in the end Joseph was blessed beyond measure and reunited with his family. God is always good and faithful.

Are You in the Wrong Circle?

To help you discern and understand the impact of being in the wrong circle of any sketchy behaviors, I want to direct you to a useful resource by Dan Drake called the Relational Circles.[55] (Learn more about this great tool on the Resources page.) Drake asks detailed and pointed questions to assist you as you become more familiar with the language of addiction.

Essentially, there are four circles—the *outer circle* (your safe place, your trusted supports), the *inner circle* (problematic sexual behaviors that have caused pain and grief), the *middle circle* (actions, emotions, and situations that are vulnerabilities or triggers), and the *relational impact* circle (positive influences (when in recovery) and negative influences (when in addiction). Once you've filled in the circles, notice the overlapping sections and what they might mean for you and your behaviors, triggers, mental states, etc.

RELATIONAL CIRCLES

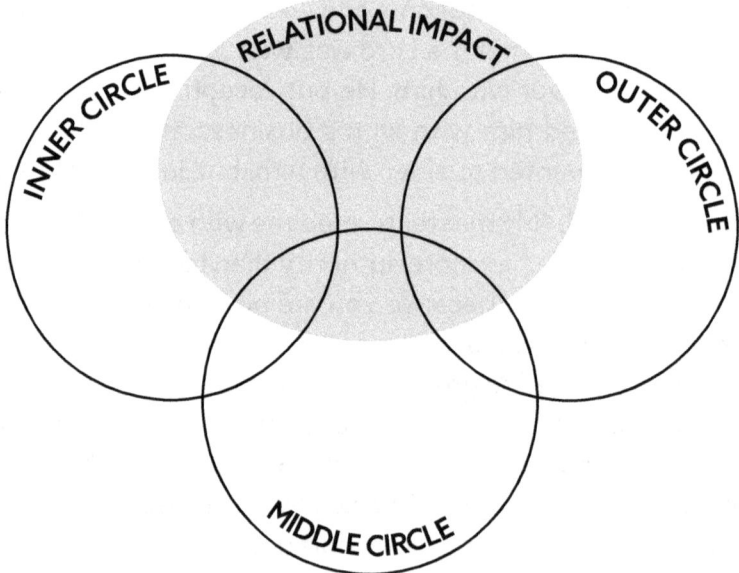

As you work through recovery, it's important to become familiar with the people, places, events, emotions, mental states, triggers, and vulnerabilities that trigger unhealthy and unsafe behaviors. This knowledge of yourself can motivate you to run toward the support systems you've worked to put into place—recovery meetings, counselors and therapists, sponsors and pastors. Even if a full relapse doesn't happen, being too close to your triggers and temptations can throw you off balance and move you further away from your recovery and higher power. Drake's questions in the Relational Circles are thought-provoking and require your honest responses to guide you through the recovery process.

Don't let the enemy have his way. It's a battle and spiritual warfare; the enemy wants to destroy all your efforts to recover. Cling to your safe space, and experience the peace and joy you get from the practice of doing the right thing. When tempted and triggered, you will need to call on an accountable person for support. Lean into the help you get from someone who has your best interests and sobriety in mind. Someone who's been there and knows the risks of falling through the cracks. Remember, you are not exempt from temptation; sin will cost you more than you want to pay, and you'll stay in it much longer than you want to visit. You are not beyond temptation.

If you have an issue with anger management and you fly off the handle because your partner wants to look at your phone, then you have a problem. Understanding what, when, and why these behaviors show up takes time and self-knowledge. Being a student of these behaviors is worth your time and energy and will likely help you avoid a relapse one day.

Maintaining Balance in Recovery

Another tool for your healing toolbox is Patrick Carne's PCI, *Personal Crazy Index*, a resource used for keeping balance in your life in recovery. There are twelve domains of sobriety, and the goal is to check in everyday to maintain balance in your life (adapted below). For success and healing, using the PCI will give you a better understanding and awareness of behaviors and old patterns that can easily creep up.[56]

The domains are physical health, transportation, home environment, work, interests, social life, family/significant others, finances, spiritual life, symptoms and behaviors, twelve-step practice, and sexuality. In each domain, you will write three unhealthy behaviors you do that keep you out of sync in that domain to maintain a healthy recovery program. Once you have your list of unhealthy behaviors, you'll choose seven behaviors to focus on shifting towards balanced and healthy habits.

I've adapted Carne's PCI below as I implement this in my practice. The goal is to track your behaviors, recognize your triggers, and then take steps to maintain balance and a healthy environment for recovery.

Balanced Behaviors Tracker

Physical Health

Your body is the temple of the Holy Spirit. It's important to take care of our vessels. If you are smoking, drinking in excess, getting too much sleep or not enough, not exercising, and eating junk food, then you are compromising your health and your body will suffer because of it. What three things do you do to jeopardize your health?

1. _____

2. _____

3. _____

Transportation

Having a car is an important part of our whereabouts—how we get there matters. Are you constantly late and having to speed up to make up lost time? Have you gotten any tickets? Are you driving your car with barely any fuel in the tank? Is your car filthy?

1. _____

2. _____

3. _____

Environment

How are you keeping up with your chores? When was the last time you cut the grass, weeded, made sure you had groceries, tending to home repairs?

1. _____

2. _____

3. _____

Work

How is your life unmanageable at work? Do you make promises that get done after deadlines? Are you returning calls, are you avoiding certain tasks, are you coming in late?

1. _____

2. _____

3. _____

Interests

What hobbies or interests do you have? Are you taking the time to explore and use your creativity? Do you make excuses to not participate? What of your interests do you not do when you are over-extended?

1. _____

2. _____

3. _____

Social Life

Think of friends in your social network who provide significant support for you, not family or significant others. When you become isolated, alienated, avoidant, or disconnected from them, what behaviors are typical of you?

1. _____

2. _____

3. _____

Family/Significant Others

What is your behavior like when you are disconnected from those closest to you? Examples are silent, overly hostile, avoidant, passive-aggressive, etc.

1. ....

2. ....

3. ....

Finances

Just as we need to manage our emotional resources to avoid becoming emotionally bankrupt, we also need to steward our financial resources. When your checking account is unbalanced, or worse, overdrawn, or bills are overdue, or there is no cash in your pocket, or you are spending more than you earn, your financial overextension may parallel your emotional bankruptcy. List the signs that show when you are financially overextended.

1. ....

2. ....

3. ....

Other Addictions or Symptom Behaviors

Compulsive behaviors have negative consequences that are symptomatic of your general well-being or overall recovery—when you watch too much television, overeat, bite your nails . . . anything you feel bad about doing afterward. Behaviors of overextension include forgetfulness, slips of the tongue, or jealousy. What damaging addictions or symptomatic behaviors do you do and know it's not good for you?

1. ....

2. ....

3. ....

Twelve-Step Practice

Living a twelve-step and recovering lifestyle involves many practices. They can be vital to staying in your healthy recovery zone when done consistently. Group attendance, step work, sponsorship, service, check-ins, accountability, and twelve-step calls become the foundation of a good recovery. Which recovery activities do you first neglect when leaving your recovery zone?

1.

2.

3.

Sexuality

For someone with sexual integrity issues, monitoring yourself sexually becomes very important. Notice if there are sexual signs that you are not doing well, feelings of shame around sexual issues, cravings, sexual aversion towards your partner, or impatient with your partner's lack of interest. Also, if there are things you may be working on to improve your sexual life, what do you notice that happens or "doesn't happen" sexually that tells you things are not going well?

1.

2.

3.

Top Seven Signs of My Personal Craziness

1. _____
2. _____
3. _____
4. _____
5. _____
6. _____
7. _____

Carnes writes, "The PCI is effective only when you are honest with yourself. It is a commitment to a very important part of your life."[59] The most important aspect of any tool is your commitment to using it. It's important to set aside time every day to check in with yourself and to build self-awareness around these behaviors. The goal is to build strong habits and a healthy foundation for a balanced life. Carnes lets us know that we should continue tracking our behaviors until we've mastered one, and then we can swap in another from the master list and focus on a new area.

I encourage you to explore Dr. Carnes' PCI a bit more with your counselor or therapist, as having this tool in your recovery toolbox will help hold you accountable as you learn to balance your life in recovery. (For further details, see the Resources page in the back of this book.)

Knowing Yourself Reveals Our Need for God

Wise leaders throughout the centuries have known that understanding our need for God begins with an understanding of our own limitations. Peter Scazzero tells us that as we begin to truly learn more about ourselves that we can then begin to discover a greater power.[57] Scazzero quotes St. Augustine as saying, "'How can you draw close to God when you are from your own self?' Augustine prayed: 'Grant, Lord, that I may know myself that I might know thee.'"[58]

CHAPTER 6: HELPING YOU HEAL

Scazzero tells us that people often die without ever fully knowing themselves. "We unconsciously live someone else's life, or at least someone else's expectations for us." This lack of self-awareness harms their relationships with others and their relationship with God.[59] The more we know of ourselves, the more we can begin to see our need for Jesus. When we're not thinking this way, we're thinking selfishly, we're focused on being right and have a self-righteous attitude, we are prideful, and our heart is not right with God. Our attitude is about having it our way. If we don't hold ourselves accountable and continue to indulge in this non-restrictive and unbridled manner, our thoughts lead to feelings of revenge and anger. Someone gets hurt. As soon as we get a hold of that part of ourselves and make things right, we can talk to it: *Where is this coming from? What are you so angry about?* We reflect and pray, "*Search my heart, Oh God, and see if there be any hurtful way in me.*" He can gently speak to our heart and lead us in the right direction. And only if we are willing to trust and allow Him to do the work of refining the impurities of our heart and attitudes will we have a changed heart and better understanding of our ways.

Nathan is another client who owns and runs a business, a place where he experienced a platform of success. He has hidden and compartmentalized behind the guise of concealing the real Nathan. He was broken, shaken, abandoned and hungered for attention. He figured out early on in life that the harder he worked for the admiration of others, the more dependent he became on fixes and people to fill him up inside. It was a false sense of security that led to his demise.

Nathan writes in a letter to his wife, "*I was constantly performing, wearing different masks to please others, but behind each mask was a person I hardly recognized. The emptiness grew, and the turmoil within became unbearable.*"[60] He took off the masks he thought were expected of him to have any value and worth and to matter as a human being. He continues, "*Owning my choices and emotions was the pivotal shift I needed. It granted me the freedom to develop personal boundaries and solidify my values around my character.*" Ultimately, for Nathan, leaning into God's grace is where he found rescue from the pain and healing. "*In faith, ownership means embracing my spiritual journey with authenticity, trusting that my relationship with God is personal and unique and founded on grace.*" I am so grateful for Nathan's hard work and his commitment to hold himself accountable to his true self.

Nathan is loved and honored in his community as a man who is in a state of self-discovery, improvement, authenticity, and loves his family and the Lord.

Allowing God to have His way in our life is far better than anything we could try and do on our own. Nathan's life moves along much better with a surrendered heart. He allows God's promptings to teach and guide him, rather than looking to man for approval. He did the hard work of searching his soul and knowing himself, and the benefits outweigh the wrong choices he's made with significant and positive outcomes. We need to check-in and ask ourselves: *Am I being respectful and kind toward others? Can I put my thoughts and feelings aside and have the capacity to hold my thoughts while another is talking? Can I ask for what I need in conversation?* How we communicate makes a world of difference to the listener.

Getting to know yourself takes time and practice. Not one of us comes from the womb knowing this relational stuff, and not many of us grew up in a home where it was modeled well. We learn primarily through trial and error and by observing those who do it well. Scazzero, in his daily calendar titled *Emotionally Healthy Spirituality Day by Day: A 40-day Journey with the Daily Office*, prays from his heart, "Holy Spirit, I invite you to dig through the layers of my being that hinder my relationships and communion with others. Grant me perseverance to allow you to dig deeply, excavating out of me all that is not of Christ so that I may be filled with your presence. In Jesus' name, amen."[61] This is a beautiful prayer we could all learn from. I love that the book of Hebrews addresses what spirituality and maturity look like for the developing man. Imagine that the following words from scripture are spoken to you personally:

> "There is much more we would like to say about this, but it's difficult to explain . . .you have been believers so long now that you ought to be teaching others. Instead, you need someone to teach you again the basics things about God's word. You are like babies who need milk and cannot eat solid food. For someone who lives on milk is still an infant and doesn't know how to do what is right. Solid food is for those who are mature, who through training have the skill to recognize the difference between right and wrong." Hebrews 5:11-15

We are to train ourselves to recognize the difference between right and wrong. I'm in my seventies now and still in progress, with still so much to learn. I thought by now I'd have it together, yet God keeps showing up and reminding us to be still and know that He is God. Taking the time to be with Him and know Him is how we allow Him to instruct and teach us about Himself and the majestic way in which He "sustains the universe by the mighty power of His command" (Hebrews 1:3).

Mother Theresa writes, "I always start my prayer in silence, for it is in the silence of the heart that God speaks . . . prayers feed the soul- and it brings you closer to God. It also gives you a clean and pure heart. A clean heart can see God, can speak to God, and can see the love of God in others."[62] It's not easy to quiet the noise and voices in our heads that tell us there's no way out or that we'll never change. But Hebrews tells us, "Since we have a great high priest who has entered heaven, Jesus the Son of God, let us hold firmly to what we believe. This High Priest of ours understands our weaknesses, for he faced all the same testings we do, yet he did not sin. So let us come boldly to throne of our gracious God. There we will receive his mercy, and we will find grace to help us when we need it most" (Hebrews 4:14-16). If you believe this, cling to it, and never stop trusting, even when your feelings and thoughts feed into lies that tell you the exact opposite of God's truth.

We will find grace and help when we ask for it. That's a promise that Jesus, the Son of God, can deliver. He is our great deliverance and higher power. He will walk you through the deepest and darkest places you will ever have to go to. "It is impossible for God to lie. Therefore, we who have fled to Him for refuge can have great confidence, as we hold to the hope that lies before us. This hope is a strong and trustworthy anchor for our souls. It leads us through the curtain of heaven into God's inner sanctuary" (Hebrews 6:18-19).

Why You're Doing the Work

Perseverance, endurance, and recovery go hand in hand; healing is a lifelong process. The apostle Paul illustrates this in 2 Timothy 2:3: "Endure suffering along with me, as a good soldier of Christ Jesus. Soldiers don't get tied up in the affairs of civilian life, for then they cannot please the officer who enlisted them." The battles we fight are spiritual wars and to get to the finish line, we follow God's ways: "Be strong through the grace that God gives you in Christ Jesus" (2 Timothy 2:1). Be ready to face adversity and "put on every piece of God's armor so you will be able to resist the enemy in the time of evil. Then after the battle you will still be standing firm. Stand your ground, putting on the belt of truth and body armor of God's righteousness" (Ephesians 6:13).

I have provided you with exercises that will help you grow, heal, better understand yourself, and give you the stamina to endure the work it takes to embrace your recovery and ultimately help your partner heal as well.

When I am most sure of myself and the path before me, it is because I have not wavered in my commitment to read and spend time in God's word. I'm at my best when I walk with Him and surrender my whole self. I have a peace that surpasses all understanding. But whenever I am inconsistent and neglect to follow through on my principles and values, I miss out on hearing what God has for me that day in his word and prayer. It's a loss of missing out on being with a Holy God who loves and desires good for me and fellowship with me as He does with you. Put Him first in your life, first thing in the morning. Read your Bible, surrender your thoughts, ways, relational circles, and recovery, and pray to become more like Him. Ask Him to help you help her heal—He can handle that kind of ask. Matthew 6:33 says, "Seek first his kingdom and his righteousness, and all these things will be given to you as well" (NIV).

Statistics and studies show that people who are intentional about their spiritual condition are healthier, happier, principled, moral and generally balanced people. The statistics below make a point to think seriously about having God as the center of your life. He is for you, not against you.

Jeff Martin from the Center of Bible Engagement researched the impact of reading Scripture extensively. He found some interesting things based on what Arnold Cole, Ed.D., and Pamela Caudill Ovwigho, Ph.D., discovered in "Understanding the Bible Engagement Challenge:

Scientific Evidence for the Power of 4." The study involved 40,000 people ages 8 to 80. Its goal was to discover if the amount of time people spent studying the scriptures made any difference in their lives. On average, up to four times a week made a tremendous difference versus one, two, or even three times a week:

1. Feeling lonely drops 30%
2. Anger issues drop 32%
3. Bitterness in relationships drops by 40%
4. Alcoholism drops 57%
5. Sex outside of marriage drops 68%
6. Feeling spiritually stagnant drops by 60%
7. Viewing pornography drops 61%
8. Sharing your faith jumps 200%
9. Discipling others jumps 230%[63]

You can't do any of this work without a daily account of who you are in Christ. He is your ultimate healer and more than anyone else He wants you to succeed. He can heal the brokenness in you. He can help you with the changes your heart has to undergo.

The word *worship* came up recently in a church service, and my mind goes right to an acronym. It helps me to remember what I want to remember about the experience. Here are some ways we can worship God as our healer and provider.

- Worship God
- Order my ways around His will for my life
- Read His word
- Sit with Him in silence
- Honor Him with my heart and mind
- Imitate Him
- Pray to Him

We need to do what the Psalmist did in Psalm 73—go into the sanctuary of God and be alone with him. This especially applies when we are surrounded by suffering and darkness. The scenes of the desert fathers come from men and women who fled to the desert as a sanctuary to seek God with their whole hearts.

Eventually, they formed communities around a "rule of life." The following are a few of the teachings they left behind. Read them slowly and prayerfully. (A "cell" was an ancient term for a quiet place to be with God.) Abba Anthony said, "Just as fish die if they stay too long out of water, the monks who loiter outside their cells or pass their time with men in the world lose the intensity of inner peace. So like a fish going towards the sea, we must hurry to reach ourselves, for fear that if we delay outside, we will lose our interior watchfulness."[64] Abbott Pastor said: "Any trial whatever that comes to you can be conquered by silence. A certain brother was sent to Abbot Moses in Scete and asked him for a good word. And the elder said to him: 'Go, sit in your cell and your cell will teach you everything.'"[65]

Our agenda and the voices in our head can sometimes prevent us from being present in prayer and seeking to know the fullness of ourselves and God in our lives. Learning to sit quietly and be still with God is a virtue. It's a practice that will change you and make you a man after God's heart. If you take this step of faith, it doesn't promise perfection and that you will never slip or relapse again, but know that He will give you all you need to endure and walk through your difficult moments. I trust and hope for you that there won't be any inner circle behaviors that would trigger inappropriate behavior. Your healing will come from putting Him first, seeking his ways, while growing in relationship with Him.

QUESTION FOR YOUR HEART

Are you all in and willing to do the work it takes to heal and restore your soul? If not, search your heart and ask yourself why.

Chapter 7

WAIT WITH EXPECTATION

"As the time of King David's death approached, he gave this charge to his son Solomon: 'I am going where everyone on earth must someday go. Take courage and be a man. Observe the requirements of the LORD your God and follow all His ways. Keep the decrees, commands, regulations, and laws written in the Law of Moses so that you will be successful in all you do and wherever you go." 1 Kings 2:1-3

We are instructed to take courage and observe God's ways that we might be "successful in all you do and wherever you go." Our human nature demands that we want it our way, and want it now. But life doesn't work that way. We need to hope for healing and set goals that are reachable and reasonable, one day at a time. You would not be expected to run a marathon overnight if you were not a runner. Patience is a virtue, and healing is something worth working for.

It takes courage to believe in yourself and make goals for yourself. What needs to happen for success to be experienced in one day, mid-week, or mid-month? Break it down into manageable expectations. For example, if I want to run and be in training for a marathon next year, what expectations need to happen by mid-year to run the course at the end of the year? And what needs to happen in the here and now to see the goal through mid-year? Perhaps some research and finding a trainer who will help and support me with my expectation to run a marathon in one year.

We're in this fight to win it. We figure out how to be in the battleground while trusting God for His help and work through us. There is a risk in all-out trusting; it may not turn out as expected. However, standing in the truth and showing up as a man who's willing to get messy, leaning into discomfort, and trusting God for the outcome, will only find favor in your partner's heart. You are in training and need to be laser-focused on your goal. You need sacrificial love, being willing to let go of something you want for something you love. Where you put your focus matters. It's foolish to think you won't struggle, but knowing to do the right thing helps us through the hard times. Just when we think we can't hang on anymore, we remember, "My help comes from the LORD, who made heaven and earth" (Psalm 121:1-2), and "the LORD Himself watches over you" (Psalm 121:5).

When the results of your efforts don't fall in your favor, there may be a tendency to check out, stop listening to the wise self, rebel against your recovery, and harden your heart. "Don't harden your hearts as Israel did when they rebelled, when they tested me in the wilderness" (Hebrews 3:8). This may be your *wilderness experience*. Expect that you will fall and rise again; you are not perfect. Put on your armor, so you can stand your ground. Be fully protected in your faith and trust in God.

Building an immunity against sin and evil is a sign of victory. You will be tested, and every scar you bear will have a story. The trials and tribulations you face and endure are not meant to hurt you but to transform your heart. Peter Scazzero quotes Gerald Sittser, saying, "The quickest way to reach the sun and the light of day is not to run west chasing after it, but to head east into the darkness until you finally reach the sunrise.[66] Proverbs 28:14 tells us that whoever hardens his heart will fall into calamity. It can feel like you're in the wilderness, all alone. Cry out to God in your loneliness, rejection, depression, and fear, like the psalmist David did, knowing that God's plan is the only way to avoid self-destruction. God tells us to return to Him: "Don't tear your clothing in your grief, but tear your hearts instead. Return to the LORD your God, for He is merciful and compassionate, slow to get angry and filled with unfailing love. He is eager to relent and not punish" (Joel 2:13).

There are many resources that come alongside you to help you through the wilderness experience. They want to see you experience success and have great expectations for your deliverance from sexual integrity issues. The Crucible Project is a program designed to challenge the obstacles that get in your way of transformation and personal change. The Men's Weekend Project challenges you to take a hard look at what you're made of, evaluating what is and isn't working in your life. The Crucible Project points you in the direction of radical honesty and unlocks a deeper level of the hidden parts of the self. If you are a man with same-sex attraction, Brother's Road offers a path to explore and support each other in aligning your sexual choices with your values, faith, and goals. Attending 90 meetings in 90 days is also a great resource. You may have to be a bit creative in finding one for each day; however, there are now a lot of meetings that meet online.

Realigning Expectations

Expectations in a marriage can be spoken and unspoken. They can either be helpful or harmful in a marriage. You might expect that your wife does the cooking, while she hates to cook. She might expect some help with the children, and you get home from work and plop yourself down on the couch. It's common to have expectations, as it is vital to communicate our needs and wants.

Unfortunately, a whole new set of expectations takes precedence in the aftermath of a discovery and disclosure. Many of the women I work with say they no longer go to beaches, watch R-rated movies or television, eat out at restaurants, or go on summer outings where women might be more exposed. They want to avoid potential triggers; they don't want to add any more pain to their lives than they are already experiencing, they don't want to be reminded of how they got in this mess, and some don't trust you or possibly themselves to manage the hurt, anger, or even rage. They're afraid that you won't have covenant eyes or bounce your eyes. She may hand you a list of expectations for emotional safety. She wants to know she has some control. At first, it can feel like a punishment for both of you. She typically will let you know her new set of expectations, but if you don't know what they are and what they mean to her, you need to ask. Remember, you're not only doing this work for your benefit, but you also get to understand on a deeper level what it costs your partner to stay in a relationship with you and work through her own pain. By putting yourself in her shoes and learning to empathize with her, you will be better equipped to make amends and put this behind you and move forward.

The following sticky note exercise is included in the workbook I've written for women, called *Spouses of Sex Addicts: Hope for the Journey Workbook*. Women used a pad of sticky notes—one note for each loss they experienced in the aftermath of their discovery and disclosure. I've done this in group settings, and they place one sticky note at a time on the wall until all their sticky notes are posted. Each woman reads her notes and tells the story behind each loss.[67] This is a difficult exercise for a partner, as she is telling her story while listening to other stories and holding her own pain. The support from other women and courage to get up and tell her story gives her a little more bravery to face her new reality. She is a beautiful warrior in a battle to get back what she's lost.

Here are some of the losses that women have stated:

- Ability to comfort me
- Confidence
- Connection
- Not being present
- Self-esteem
- Lost my worth
- Feel old and damaged
- Stability
- Family
- Future
- Sexual energy
- Loyalty, standing up for me
- Being true to me
- Protecting and honoring us
- Not being enough
- Respect

- Relaxed to hyper-vigilant
- No peace
- Health
- The reality of knowing who he is
- Innocence
- Trust
- Honesty
- Companionship
- Circle of friends and activities
- Financial security
- Career
- Romance
- Loss of self
- Peace of mind
- Commitment
- Confidence in men
- Loss of a dream
- Love
- Loss of champion, best friend
- Security
- Sleep
- Laughter
- Intimacy
- Travel
- Retirement together

This incomplete list provides a perspective on why you are working on redoing, remaking, rebuilding, recovering, and recreating your relationship with your partner. Your wife may not relate to everything on this list, but I'm pretty sure she could identify with quite a few.

There is healing in telling our stories. As women become more and more aware of their feelings, they start to heal and notice what they need to know and understand about themselves and how courageous they've become in facing many of their hardships in this process. They can stay connected to themselves, have clearer thoughts, understand their behaviors, and better process their grief.

Even after some healing, it doesn't take much to set triggers off; the last thing your partner needs is to feel the competition of a woman at the beach and imagine what you might be thinking. Be mindful of your behavior and her heart. In time, as you wait in expectation, you will have the opportunity to speak about your needs. "In the morning, Lord, you hear my voice; in the morning I lay my requests before you and wait in expectation" (Psalm 5:3). Waiting with expectation for God to work and do something in our lives is different than waiting and being ridden with anxiety or frustration that things aren't going our way. Waiting with our hearts laid out before God, with great expectation of what He is doing through us and in us is spiritual maturity and personal growth.

It's worth the effort to have a plan and conversation with your partner about private and public expectations. At the beginning of my discovery journey, when we were in public, I wanted my husband to hold my hand and reassure me that he had covenant eyes. In private, I expected a daily check-in and complete honesty. The man I married fifty-three years ago has had a change of heart. I don't have to remind him. He loves me with a new and tender heart, for which I am grateful and thankful for.

Set Expectations with a New Covenant

One of the ways you can reposition yourself and your expectations as a man in recovery is to write out a covenant. It is not a legal document, but a written agreement of the expectations of your behaviors and consequences if you fall short of following through. By writing this out, you are letting your partner know exactly what she can expect from you moving forward. After you have prayed over it, searched your heart, and reviewed the details with your partner, you should sign the agreement. (For help writing your own covenant, you can find a sample template on my website. Please visit the Resources page at the end of this book for more information.)

When you outline boundaries and consequences for violating your promises, both you and your partner have clear expectations, the pressure is removed in the moment should you cross a boundary line, and you are able to take responsibility for your actions immediately. As an example of what consequences might look like if you are struggling with viewing pornography, you might consider more frequent meetings, accountability, treatment, or whatever it takes to be safe, sober, healthy, and honest. It's also important to remember that consequences won't always leave room for reconciliation or second chances, and that could be hard to accept.

I understand how hard it is for you to make a promise of this nature. Saying that you will never act out again is a hard thing to say; many men worry, *"What if I do? Then I'm even more of a liar and addict to her."* As hard as it can be to stay sober, believe with all your heart that you are free of this addiction and that there won't be any middle or inner circle behaviors. Believe in yourself. If you slip or relapse, make amends right away. Don't waste time denying or rationalizing. Tell your sponsor and therapist. Find a way to tell your partner.

I asked my husband what kept him from going back to his old behaviors, and he answered, *"I hate that part of my life, who I was, how secretive and hurtful I was to you."* I know you don't want to tear her heart out again, and it hurts your heart to think you could ever go back there again after promising her she is safe with you. The impact letter she wrote to you after disclosure, as she understood the pain of your betrayal, can be good to read every now and then as a reminder of why you choose to be safe, sober, honest, and healthy every day.

The covenant assures her and gives her hope, something she desperately seeks as she has her eyes on you. The signed covenant with its included consequences speaks to how you know what she needs to feel safe. She wants you to know and understand that you could tear her heart open again if you fail to follow through and keep your word. It gives her peace of mind knowing you are owning up and taking responsibility for your behaviors. She did not cause them, can't cure them, and can't control them. Partners have often asked me, *"What consequences should I give him if he . . . ?"* She should not have to take on the responsibility of assigning consequences or controlling the outcome. Putting the responsibility of policing you on her is an easy cop-out for you and a distraction from her own healing process.

A Reflective Heart

Below is a letter my husband wrote me in a time of repentance and a reflective heart. He acknowledged the hurt and took full responsibility for his actions. I believe in the power of prayer, and in my heart, I know that Dan's change of heart can only come from desiring and believing himself that God could turn his life around. I waited with expectation that God would break through the walls he put up and wrestle with God till he finally surrendered his whole heart and life.[68]

This letter is evidence of his own reflections of his actions and ability to be in touch with his feelings; I did not ask him to write this letter. He has worked hard to earn my trust back. We have worked hard together to renew our hearts and minds as one in Christ.

> *"To the angel of my youth, my beloved bride of over fifty years,*
>
> *My heart grieves and torments over my behaviors and attitudes that were compiled from ungodly influences. I am writing this note to you from the depths of my soul and from the bottom of my heart. I say to you now that I am so very, very sorry for my narcissism and behaviors that hurt you, my ungodly attitudes, my selfishness, my entitlement, my expectations, the words and thoughts I have spoken to you verbally and nonverbally. I'm in my 70s now and God has been molding and shaping me as he did with Moses. I feel the torment in my soul for this journey that involves hurting you and taking away the joy and the pressure I put on you. I am so very sorry; you didn't deserve the monster inside of me that took joy and pleasure from you. I am thankful to God that he has gotten my attention over the years; I've built too many walls; I had pride when I should have been convicted of driving at the speed that makes you feel comfortable after many years of you asking me to slow down. The expectations I put on you for my sexual gratification needs were selfish and all about what I wanted. I am so sorry for the pain I caused you those many years. I can't fully explain nor try to justify my behaviors. I take total responsibility for my actions and truly apologize for the pain I caused you. You are a beautiful woman whom God chose to be a part of my life*

and molding and shaping me; I am so thankful that you are my wife. I didn't deserve you. God felt that you are the one for me, for life to touch, to hold, to cherish, and that's what I want to do from the bottom of my heart. I will pray that this old person, as described above, will no longer surface his head. You are an amazing woman, kind, loving, and selfless, putting me first in all the years of our life together; you are indeed an angel sent from God to work with the confused young man I was, so that I could blossom into a man of God, whom you can admire, adore, and love always, without fear of judgment. Again, I can't tell you enough how sorry and irresponsible I was for my actions and behaviors and the pain I caused you."

I appreciate the time, prayer, and changes my husband has put into becoming a man after God's heart. He has looked deeply into his himself to know and understand the ways of his heart, purging the old and developing the man God meant for him to be. In many ways, he is a new man. I love being with him and sharing life with him. I fell in love with a young man who was protective of my heart and interested in knowing me and being known. He wanted to study the word of God and serve Him. As he has become the man he is today, I love that we pray together first thing every morning for our family and friends. I look forward to waking up and spending time with my best friend and the love of my life; I know I matter by the intentions of his heart to make our relationship a priority. The journey God allowed us to experience was meant to grow us and make us more like Him. It wasn't an illness or death but sexual integrity issues, and it took us through the wilderness and crucible experience, where we both had to die to self and open our hearts to God. He purged the *uglies* we both had in us, made us bigger, stronger, and more in love with each other than we've ever been. On August 19, 2025, we will celebrate our fifty-third wedding anniversary.

I read somewhere that the best apology is a changed behavior. Your partner will notice when you take ownership and address the consequences of your sexual integrity issues. As I have written, my husband's sexual indiscretion was pornography. Still, after reading his letter, you may have noticed he wrote that he was narcissistic, selfish, prideful, and had an ungodly attitude. This is what drove him because of his underlying wounds, and that is what broke my heart. We are making up for lost time;

we have grieved the moments that sin robbed us of and restored what was stolen in the making of a healthy, loving relationship. We say we have *overcome* and are on the other side of the wall. We cannot do this without God as the center of our hearts and marriage. In Zechariah 2:5, God says, "Then I, myself, will be a protective wall of fire around Jerusalem." To me, that scripture is saying that He is our wall; He protects us from predators who aim to take our joy and destroy us. "Anyone who harms you harms my most precious possession" (Zechariah 2:8). Life is precious, and we have much to be thankful for. If, in our younger years, we had the tools I'm giving you, I'd like to say it would have made a big difference for my husband and me, but honestly, I don't know that. You are given the tools, and I hope that using the covenant and writing out what you will do to keep her safe will help you become the man she wants and needs you to be and the man you believe in. God has been cutting away at my pride and teaching me to forgive, be more like Him, and throw away judgments as far as the East is from the West. I can't say I'm thankful for this journey, but I am thankful that God has had his hand on both of us, holding our hearts, teaching us what it cost Him for our sin, and what it means for us to live for Him, and to love like Him. Living with a man who has been broken and cleaned up for the Lord, humbled himself before God and others, has encouraged my spirit and heart to be more Christ-like.

QUESTION FOR THE HEART

Can you say: "I do acknowledge that I must always work to prove myself trustworthy and to provide a place in our home and in my heart where you will feel loved, protected and cherished as my wife."? If you are not at that point, what is holding you back?

Chapter 8

BE OF A SOBER MIND: LONG-TERM HEALING

"Do not be anxious about anything, but in every situation by prayer and petition with thanksgiving, present your requests to God. And the peace of God which transcends all understanding, will guard your hearts and your minds in Christ Jesus." Philippians 4:5-7 (NIV)

We live in perilous times. We are a people under stress and demands and different from any other time. Not only is this in our personal lives, but in our culture, work, financially, and health wise with almost every corner we turn. We were never promised a rose garden. But life can be hard for a time or a season. It is crucial for you to understand how to hold up as you take on more work that recovery requires of you and help your partner heal. The Bible tells us to be on the alert, to pray always, and to be of a sober mind. We are not to allow the ways of the world to distract and influence our focus, but to think clearly and exercise self-control. To behave in the way of a sound mind, diligent, disciplined, alert to the dangers of falling prey to evil, consistent and predictable. That's what Jesus was and that's who we want to model after.

It is too easy to drift, fall away, and forget the promises we have in God. "Don't slip back into your old ways of living . . . you didn't know any better then" (1 Peter 1:14).

We are creatures of habit; what feels comfortable and familiar wants to draw us back to the same old survival patterns. If you're not taking time each day to be with Jesus, learning what it means to be more like him, and giving him your prayer request with a thankful heart, you are losing out and risk falling back into temptation. He wants to be your best friend. He doesn't want to see you fail. He hurts when you hurt. He desires to be in a relationship with you. You are unique to Him. He wants you to have the desires of your heart as you seek what He wants for you, and His will for your life. Being of sober mind means being serious, "So be on your guard, not asleep like the others. Stay alert and be clearheaded" (1 Thessalonians 5:6). The Bible tells us to be a prepared people, be on the alert, and to be watchful for any impending situations that may be coming down the pike. That kind of readiness means having clarity and the presence of mind to not sway from the things that are good and pure and have a focus on eternal value.

Becoming is sober-minded, a freedom walk, living under God's influence and grace with eternity in view. It not only changes you mentally, emotionally, and spiritually, but it gives you clarity by living with a clear mind and focusing on your recovery. "Prepare your minds for action and exercise self-control" (1 Peter 1:13). The late Mark Lasser describes some of his darkest moments as "being confronted with depression, anguish, getting punched in the stomach with some bad news."[69]

Experiencing such pain—whether emotional, physical, or spiritual—demands alertness and a mind that requires a presence of calm, composed and a collected sense of self and character traits. Some of the men I know in recovery have held fast and furious to the point of exhaustion, and yet are still holding on. They are hoping and praying for healing as they purge the erratic and insensible behaviors that contributed to the addiction.

Laaser also talks about a course correction: "If we don't allow God to leave us with the pain we're going through, we won't experience the vision improvement.[70] We have to "get up," as Jesus told his disciples, and stay awake and watch with me for even one hour. Keep alert and pray—otherwise, the temptation will overpower you.

I recently found a letter that speaks to the pain of a partner in the *cup of suffering* from an anonymous woman on the SA Lifeline Foundation blog. (Please refer to the Appendix for more information regarding this anonymous letter and for more details about incredible work of the SA Lifeline Foundation.) This anonymous woman, in her darkest moments, allowed the course to correct itself and to redirect and transform her life.[71] In her vulnerable writing, she speaks to friends and family about what she wishes they knew about her pain and silent suffering. She begins her plea with: *"I desperately need you to see me, because I am silently drowning . . ."* and she continues to share her heart and experiences, in hopes that her support network can begin to have a better understanding of the seriousness of sexual addiction induced trauma (SAIT). In the end, after she's poured her heart out, explained her need throughout to be seen and understood, she finally shares: *"The Savior I always believed in has extended me mercy. God's grace saved me and became very real to me. I talk to Him often, and even though you don't see me, I know that He does."* When she felt she had nowhere else to go, she put her trust in God and believed He would heal her *whole mind, body, and soul*. I encourage you to look up the letter and then reflect on the following questions. Write your responses in your journal:

- What am I feeling after reflecting and reading this letter a second time?

- I didn't realize the depth of pain my partner had in the area of
_____.

Sober mindedness requires an understanding of what you want with the knowledge and wisdom of seeking God's truth. My hope is that one day you also will say, "This is the catalyst I needed to finally find myself, to discover the beautiful and amazing hidden parts of yourself that you hadn't noticed before." Get to know yourself and the parts of you that hurt and discover the beautiful and amazing parts of you that are yet to be discovered.

I watched the movie *The Blind*, the life story of Phil Robertson, the Duck Dynasty reality TV star. The horrors and trauma of his childhood led to the fallout of a self-destructive lifestyle. His demons haunted and pursued him through mood-altering drugs, ripping him to shreds and losing every good thing in his life. The lure of taking his childhood pain away seemed so glamorous and inviting until he barely knew who he was anymore. His wife left him and took a step of faith, trusting God to provide for her and the children, while Phil struggled on his own, facing the discomfort necessary and needed to tolerate, wash away, and put away once and for all the self-destructing behaviors. Phil differentiated from the hopeless, helpless self and saw himself as he was and had been in his addiction, to how he could be empowered by giving his life to Jesus. This is a decision we all need to make for ourselves.

Talking Back to Your Addiction

You need to learn how to talk back to your addiction and get familiar with its many voices, sounds, smells, and triggering situations, because your addiction doesn't want you to experience success. You must speak directly to your addiction, out loud or in your head if you have to, "NO, NOT TODAY! You have no power over me!" The apostle John wrote in 1 John 4:4, "The Spirit who lives in you is greater than the spirit who lives in the world." The Spirit of Christ living in you empowers you to talk back and walk away from your addiction.

Memorizing scripture is your most potent tool against the tactics of the evil one. Satan shudders at the name of Jesus. Colossians 1:11–12 will equip you with empowering words in a moment you need them most: "We also pray that you will be strengthened with all His glorious power so you will have all the endurance and patience you need. May you be filled with joy, always thanking the Father, who has enabled you to share in the inheritance that belongs to God's holy people, who live in the light."

In my practice, I've found Patrick Carnes' Core Dialogue exercise to be an incredibly helpful program. You can find this exercise in his Recovery Starter Kit book, and this forty-day practice is intended to be conversation between *the recovering you* and *the you that gave in to lust*. In Carnes' exercise, you are the man in recovery who is no longer powerless but working on your sobriety and a healthy recovery program ("I") and you will be in dialogue with the addictive part of you that took over your life ("you").[72] It's a battle between good and evil, and gives you the power to experience victory in your recovery process. Each day focuses on a different area of the 10 Core Dialogue Queries (CDQ): Denial, Relationships, Life Patterns, Relapse, Multiple Addictions, Unresolved Issues, My Ability to

Have Feelings, My Ability to Commit, the Role of Crisis in my Life, and the way I Self-Sabotage. For example, the first day focuses on the topic of Denial and asks you to reflect on how the addiction came to be and why it started and gives you space to answer a hard question: "What have I not wanted to face about you being in my life?" The second day allows you to reflect on relationships and asks: "Who in my family has most affected your addiction?" and " Is there anyone who benefits from my addiction?" At the end of each week, you assess your progress for that week in each area of the core dialogue queries. It's important that you share your progress and ask for help throughout with a trusted group member or your therapist. (For further details and information on how to access the Core Dialogue exercise, please see the Resources page in the back of this book.)

If you seek out this exercise and complete all forty days, you should end with a better understanding of your addiction, how it has purposed and served you, and how it makes you feel about yourself when it's around. The knowledge you gain about yourself can be shared with your counselor, therapist or at group meetings. I'd love to hear if any of your answers surprised you and if you were able to identify any patterns in your behaviors. It is essential to know how the addictive part of you evolved and grew to be out of control. When you become aware of its compulsion and know how it sneaks its way back and deceives you, you are better equipped to say, "No, not now, not today; I won't cave into your evil ways that rob me of time and family and keep me locked in shame and isolation."

After working through the Core Dialogue Queries, Reed, my client, had a better understanding of how many aspects of his life had been taken from him by addiction. His addiction to pornography and the subsequent downward spiral when his secrets and lies were found out had destroyed his life, and Reed worked hard to rebuild and gain trust again as he began to unravel the origins of his addiction, the triggers, and healthy ways to work through his pain.[73]

> *"To my addiction:*
>
> *I am writing an assignment to say goodbye to you. I should have done this years ago after allowing you so many years to take the reins in my life. Over two years ago, my wife discovered the stash of pornography that I hid in our basement; I felt relief and yet so afraid and ashamed that she would take our family and leave me."*

Reed's father died when he was young and his mom was dealing with her own pain, so when Reed found a stash of magazines in the school dumpster at the age of twelve, he learned to hide his pain, found comfort in escaping, and believe the lie of addiction that he could keep this secret from those he loved. Reed's addiction to pornography affected him throughout his college years, as he spent more and more time seeking escape.

> *"You made it seem so exciting and convincing at every corner I turned and that there was more, bigger and better. I hate you for that. I hate that I gave you so much power and control. It was like you became a part of my DNA. The first thing I did in the morning was look at pornography. I lived for it, and it was the last thing I did at the end of the day."*

In his letter, Reed confronts the pain his addiction brought to his life and the lies he told his wife, Maggie, before they married. Reed became manipulative and deceitful as his lies and secrets pushed a deeper wedge between him and Maggie. Reed describes the look of disappointment from his young son. "I have to finish a project," he'd reply when asked to play catch with him in the yard. There were more lies and more cover ups when money from the family budget was stolen to support his addiction and chat room subscriptions.

Reed explains that his addiction taught him well to lie and deceive and assured him his secrets would not be found out. He details that Maggie never suspected what he was hiding from, and that he regrets how much of his life he missed by escaping to the world of fantasy and pornography and allowing his heart to be hardened with shame and worthlessness.

> *"I grieved as a grown man for my dad; I had not ever cried like that. Mom had her pain, but I realized that I had to forgive her for not being there for me, and for not getting me the help I needed as a young boy who had just lost his dad and best friend. I cried for my wife, the pain and trauma she experienced at discovery, the lies I told her, and how she innocently believed me."*

Reed ends his letter by telling his addiction that he no longer fears that he wants nothing to do with it. He acknowledges the poison took over and he knows that between meetings, accountability, and counseling, his eyes are open to the pain he has caused through his addiction. Reed says that "the visual exercise of throwing his addiction as far as possible into the woods" was incredibly helpful in letting go and separating his life from his addiction. He's reaching deep within his heart for the strength to continue his path to healing and rebuilding the relationships around him.

> *"So, goodbye addiction, I want nothing to do with you; everything you touch and seductively whisper to your takers is poisonous. I no longer fear you. I no longer need you or want you anywhere near me.*
>
> *Reed"*

Only by God's grace and strength can someone write a goodbye letter of such. Reed was of a sober mind writing to his addiction; he took his assignment to heart and wanted a lasting change. He paid attention to his timeline, and how addiction took on a life of its own, and how it had its way with him. Reed drank the cup of suffering. He understood what it meant to sit in it and get to the other side of his painful memories so that he could experience the grace and peace that surpasses all understanding. Thankfully he was able to say, *"I needed to finally find myself, to discover the beautiful and amazing hidden parts of myself that I never got to know because the addiction kept me self-absorbed and isolated from the real me."* God wants us to understand and know ourselves "We ask God to give you a complete understanding of what He wants to do in your lives and we ask Him to make you wise with spiritual wisdom" (1 Colossians 1:9).

QUESTION FOR YOUR HEART

Can you write a goodbye letter to your addiction? While there's no perfect way to do this, you could start with how the addiction impacted you. Be specific, and write what you are doing about that impact now.

Chapter 9

RADICAL LOVE AND TRANSFORMATION

"Greater love has no one than this, to lay down one's life for one's friend." John 15:13 (NIV)

In Matthew 22:39 we are commanded to love our neighbor as we love ourselves. That is radical. It's not easy to love others when they are clearly being obstinate, unloving, and unforgivable. And we certainly have it in us to be the same way, yet it's only through God's grace that we can love in the way He desires for us. "I beg you to lead a life worthy of your calling . . . for you have been called by God. Always be humble and gentle. Be patient with each other, making allowance for each other's faults because of your love" (Ephesians 4:1-3). That is radical love, a shift and transformation to love our neighbors as we love ourselves. We can only genuinely love others when we accept God's love for ourselves. "May you experience the love of Christ, though it is too great to understand fully. Then you will be made complete with all the fullness of life and power that comes from God" (Ephesians 3:19). It's impossible to love others in a way that is "worthy of our calling" unless we accept who we are in Christ and put our trust in God. He sees in us through the blood of our Savior Jesus.

Restoration is a radical part of the recovery process. Only because of the work at the cross can we experience the greatness of His love that empowers us to love and forgive ourselves. We "no longer do as the Gentiles do, for they are hopelessly confused. Their minds are full of darkness; they wander far from the life God gives because they have shut their minds and hardened their hearts against Him" (Ephesians 4:17-18). We have unlimited resources and a mighty and fearless inner strength that comes from the powers of God. We are told not to despair, not give up, because He purchased our freedom and because He showered kindness on us and forgives our sins; we are blessed with all wisdom and understanding. We are challenged in every direction of our lives to put on and practice using this incredible gift of love we've been given. It is just as hard to love radically as it is to sit in misery. James 5:13 tells us to love one another, carry each other's burdens, and confess our sins to one another. We can't love like that on our own, but we can do it together. I love what my pastor preached one Sunday morning, saying, *"You can expose it in the light, or Satan will beat you down in the dark."* We all wrestle with sin, and not one of us is perfect. In the trials and tribulations of our lives, we most need each other's love and encouragement. Satan wants nothing more than to remind us of our mistakes, he wants to keep us groping in the past: and miss the opportunities right before us. 1 Peter 4:12 tells us not to be surprised at what lies before us, "Don't be surprised at the fiery trials you are going through, as if something strange is happening to you." Some of our best moments come from putting on God's armor and speaking out in our bravest moments through the trials we've had to endure and come out on the other side of it. On that same Sunday morning, Pastor also shared a story about an elder in our church who had been a football player and spent the last twenty years of his life in a wheelchair. The football player stated that he had learned more about himself and life than he had at any other time of his life. An elder now, he pours his out his heart and love from his wheelchair, radically loving on the church.

"It is a lifestyle shift which brings together different ideas, values and principles that are counter cultural and challenge society."[74] A lifestyle shift is radical authenticity when you understand your purpose and intent to love yourself and serve others with radical genuineness.

We can be especially hard on ourselves and others when something of them is mirrored back at us. Making a conscious effort to listen and be attentive to break down any barriers and walls that are making it impossible to shift to an open heart, "doesn't happen often to people who break easily, or have sharp edges, or who have to be carefully kept."[75] Using the acronym S.T.O.P. is a good reminder to slow yourself down and turn things around when you're impatient or not feeling humble and kind to yourself or others: *Stop, Think, Open, Pray.*

At times, I can be so hard on myself: *"You can't write a book! You don't know what you're doing. No one is going to read it, so why bother?"* If I complain to someone, in their effort to encourage me; I doubt them. That's not living worthy of my calling to be humble and kind. I'm wasting an opportunity for growth and emotional development. God wants to teach me and hold me accountable for all of what He has poured into me. Do you recall what happens when we allow destructive thoughts to linger; the limbic brain system interprets our negative thoughts as a threat. The prefrontal cortex starts to shut down, and we're not thinking with our best interests in mind. Remember Daniel Siegel's hand model? What our brain perceives as a warning diverts to the limbic brain, which takes over and functions in a threatening situation and our capacity to think and reason on our behalf is compromised.

Protect your brain from negative thoughts; when you get stuck in that mindset, it can lead to depression and anxiety, and it can also compromise your immune system. This is where using the ABCDE model we discussed in Chapter 4 can be helpful. You have an activating triggering event, which gets filtered through your belief system, resulting in consequences, feelings and emotions, which you can then dispute, and exchange for a different and radical belief. For example, if you find yourself thinking, *"I made a mistake. I spoke out of line. I will never learn. I do this all the time. I'm so mad at myself,"* you can dispute those thoughts with, *"I don't always do this; I'm a good person."* And exchange your thoughts: *"I can apologize, I will slow myself down in emotionally charged conversations, and speak my truth with assertiveness, not aggression. I will take deep breaths and control my thoughts and feelings. I will be attentive to what I say to myself."*

Checking for Self-Destructive Talk and Behaviors

Some of the more harmful ways of not loving yourself are connected to your sexual integrity issues. The work you do to acquire a change of heart will require patience and alternative solutions, considering what it might look like to do differently from what is known and familiar to you. "Be on guard. Stand firm in the faith. Be courageous. Be strong. And do everything with love" (1 Corinthians 16:13,14). A radical is someone who has very extreme views and ideas. Radical love is a major shift from *"it's all about me"* to *"everything you do must be done with a spirit of love and humility."* It's being purposeful about what you do with your life and energy and requires an intention to choose to move away from destructive habits and lifestyles that are hurtful to others.

I have another acronym for you as a self-check and a deliberate shift in your thinking and behavior to a conscious state of mind. Pay attention and see if there be any self-destructive talk or behaviors that you connect with in this acronym. Use DANGLER as a guide as you reflect on your day in a daily check-up: Denial, Anger, Negative Self-Talk, Gaslighting, Lying, Egomania, and Rationalizing. The key to having these tools work is to practice and use them.

Denial

Denial is hurtful not only to others but also to yourself. If you refuse to accept someone else's reality based on a behavior or thought you imposed on them, you discount them and minimize their reality, as well as denying your own capability to accept the possibility of someone else being in the right. Slow down to understand and ask questions for clarity. Choose growth by being willing to do the work it takes to own up, make an amendment, apologize, or clear up any misconceptions. Your ideas and thoughts can be taken seriously and respectfully as you listen to understand the heart and ways of another. Find something in their story that makes sense to you. Be the best of you, and show up with humility, patience and kindness.

Anger

Anger can appear in the form of an outright aggressive response or even a violent reaction to being wrong, losing control, retaliation, unbridled self-expression, withdrawing out of fear, being passive-aggressive, not knowing or fully understanding the circumstances, not feeling understood, feeling taken advantage of, not feeling heard, thinking someone is withholding or withdrawing from you. These are just a few ways anger shows up, and indeed, some of these expressions can have justification, but only when handled in love. But it is never the case for justification towards abusive behavior. This is where you S. T. O. P. Slow yourself down, take deep breaths, and communicate your needs in a loving and respectful manner.

Negative Self-Talk

Get your facts, do your research, and turn away from any negative conversations you have with yourself that could trigger middle or inner-circle behaviors. Fear is our biggest culprit, accusing us of our wrong doings and limiting our potential. Be prepared: when you start to feel these critical attacks coming on, whether it's the inner critic or from someone else, your brain is fired up to respond to the threat. Don't listen to the criticism, but instead use your tools to overcome the negativity. You must exchange the old negative thoughts and patterns of the way and manner you talk to yourself. Otherwise, the false accusations take on a life of their own, and you become what you think, since we are highly influenced by our thoughts.

Gaslight

Gaslighting is a term partners use when they feel like they're being tricked. It's a form of psychological abuse. It distorts her reality, what she knows and believes as truth. She begins to question herself, and her intuition is often the first to go. Be aware of how you deny, manipulate the truth, lie, don't own up, only think of yourself, and make her look like the perpetrator. In reality, you are controlling the outcome and demanding power over your partner—and that too is psychological abuse.

Lies

You've heard the phrase: *"You're only as sick as your secrets."* The lies you tell yourself and persuade others to believe will only turn around and hurt you. It can be painful, humiliating, humbling, and scary to disclose and be vulnerable, especially if your partner is right, or when you know that confessing might mean taking a step backward. Remember, you are doing the right thing by owning up and telling her the truth. It may hurt for a while, but there's freedom in pursuing the truth. It starts with being honest with yourself, others, and your heavenly Father. Don't buy into the lies that Satan would want you to believe: "He was a murderer from the beginning. He has always hated the truth because there is no truth in Him. When he lies, it is consistent with his character; for he is a liar and the father of lies" (John 8:44).

Egomania

The ego says, *"It's all about me, my party, my way."* The focus is on self: *"I'm the greatest and most important. I want what I want and when I want it."* An egomaniac is self-absorbed and truly believes they matter more than anyone else. They do whatever it takes to get what they want.

Egomaniacs often push their own thoughts and ideas on their partners. They demand change for their own benefit in an aggressive and harmful way. Partners want nothing to do with this. They want to run as far as possible from this egregious conduct. Your partners know and sense when your defenses are impacting them; they do not feel safe. They can sense when the tone of your voice escalates, your posture stiffens, and your face and neck tighten. These actions speak clearly and let them know they are not safe or secure. Take ownership, make amends, do the loving thing, love radically, shift gears, and tell the old tapes they are not welcome here. There is no room for the self-centered self! The sooner you make an honest and loving amends, the better it is for you and your partner.

Rationalize

Rationalization can be subtle and sneaky as we justify our behaviors, feelings, and thoughts. The sad part is we convince ourselves and explain it away as though we are dogmatically correct and logical. Pathological liars believe the fantasy and stories they construct and have the tendency to live in that world, and that doesn't have to be you. Be genuine and take a moment to be deliberate, plan to go well, internalize it, own and live in the truth of who you know yourself to be. Tony Gaskins reminds us, "Many would rather believe a lie because the truth requires a change."[76]

If you use the DANGLER acronym as part of a consistent check-in, you'll notice a shift in your mental state and in the way you talk to yourself. The consistent check-in will hold you accountable and will allow you to interact with your surroundings from a place of reflection instead of reaction. Terry Real's "Five Winning and Losing Strategies" will give you hope. He explains the do's and don'ts that matter and make a huge difference in how you love and respond to your partner.[77] The losing strategies explain how we get stuck in the DANGLER acronym and set ourselves up to lose. When you get stuck in losing strategies, you fail to negotiate, compromise, learn from your mistakes, and explore other creative options. Engaging in losing strategies leaves no room for radical love as an option for a higher calling of a better self.

These strategies are an outline to guide you through winning and losing strategies for communicating effectively. Remember that it's important to pause before interacting or starting a conversation with your partner. Have you considered how the conversation will affect your partner? Remember your love for your partner, and choose an approach that will heal and not harm them.

Losing strategies in relationships stem from behaviors that encourage a lack of trust, disrespect, and work to break emotional connection. This might happen when you are overly focused on being right, which creates arguments over which perspective is more accurate or might fuel a feeling of superiority. Controlling your partner through manipulation will lead to resentment and retaliation as no one enjoys feeling controlled. Speaking your mind without kindness or respect can be hurtful and damaging. Retaliation, whether through direct or passive-aggressive actions, comes from taking on a victim mindset and aims to make the other person feel the same pain. Lastly, withdrawal further erodes the relationship as it only creates more distance.

Winning strategies focus on love, respect, and effective communication to further strengthen relationships. One key approach is to shift from constant complaining to clearly expressing what you need in a specific and reasonable manner. When you work to repair with love and respect, you engage in intentional dialogues or conversations that will prioritize understanding and connection. It's important to share what you saw and heard, what you made up about it, how you feel about it, and what you'd like—this approach provides a structured way to communicate your emotions constructively. Finally, letting go of the outcome and listening with compassion encourages a focus on mutual respect and growth within the relationship. This allows each party to feel empowered and respected.[78]

Any time you converse or have any kind of interaction with each other remember the winning and losing strategies and do the work to utilize winning strategies to create a healthier dynamic in your interactions.

Avoid Triggers

Whether you're doing DANGLER, Losing and Winning Strategies, or any other tool I've given you, know that you will need to ask yourself some hard questions when you start to feel out of control—*start to feel* is the key here. If your emotions and behaviors are already out of control, it's not too late, but it will require more effort to remember and use your skills. Triggers can pop up all over the place and leave you feeling helpless. Be prepared. Ask yourself these important questions: Am I in denial about something? Am I angry? Am I talking negatively to myself or others? Am I manipulating, gaslighting, or lying? Is my ego larger than life right now, or am I rationalizing the truth? Am I in any middle circle behaviors right now? Am I in danger of being Hungry, Angry, Lonely, or Tired (HALT)—an acronym commonly used in 12-step programs? Any of these stressors can set you up for a slip or relapse. You have worked way too hard to lose your sobriety. It's worth the effort to slow down, take deep breaths, and do a self-assessment.

Please don't bring any defensive strategies with you; leave them at the door behind you. It's liberating to recognize the good work you're doing and empowering when you can self-correct. Be gentle with yourself, and be patient if you have a hard time understanding where your partner is at. She truly wants you to know her heart and pain. Be curious while staying attentive and listening to her heart. She wants to help you and be supportive of the work and changes she sees in you. When you know the depth of the pain she's in, you become better at being empathic. Suspend any beliefs you may be suspicious of, as in thinking she's exaggerating or making things up. Be willing to unpack any misconceptions about the situation at hand. Be teachable, be kind, and be respectful.

Ellen and her husband separated while he sought out therapy for his addiction issues. She writes that the separation was incredibly hard and emotional for everyone involved. Suddenly, she was managing parenting her kids on her own, while also dealing with the financial burden.[79] This was a difficult position to find herself in and she didn't have the support she needed to navigate the changes and stress she was encountering because of her husband's therapy and treatment.

While she knew therapy would help, she also felt like something was wrong—her husband no longer had to deal with his responsibilities in the house and family but everything now fell on her to sustain. Ellen needed protection for her heart and the desperation to be heard, understood, and supported. She needed her husband to love her without any of the losing strategies on board. She needed a man who was not afraid to change and love radically:

> *"Who will put me together again? I prayed and asked God to get rid of this pain in my heart, it hurt so badly. What did I ever do to receive this pain? Why did He allow me to marry such a deceitful person? I was also mad at myself for being taken as a fool."*

It can be hard to communicate these feelings of isolation and the need for additional support. When we're faced with a difficult situation where one partner needs help, it can feel like the other partner just needs to take on everything else without question. It's important to be able to rely on each other, trust that each person will keep their promises for support, and to also ensure we have a supportive community to lean on and be honest with in times of need.

Another of Terry Real's useful tools is a question he poses that is meant to help and support your needs: *"What can I give you or do for you to help you give me what I need?"*[80] I appreciate the depth of this statement; it works well when both of you want healing and recovery to restore what's been lost. For example: you want to plan a weekly date with your partner, both to spend time with her and rekindle some trust and dependability. She has a hard time believing you will follow through, and when you ask what she needs from you to make the date happen, she responds with the following: *"I would like you to line up the babysitter, watch the children and feed them while I take a shower."* Now, it is your job to follow through and show up in the way she needs. This question works both ways, and suppose she asks you to go to a marriage weekend retreat with her, and you respond, *"I need to know at the end of the retreat what your commitment level is to our marriage, and what you're willing to do or not for the sake of our relationship."* You have asked her to help you get what you need.

You're the man who wants to help her heal. It's important to be mindful of your ways and how you show up. Respond, and present as a man who is in the process of *becoming*. You are not perfect, but be willing to have a teachable heart. "Never let loyalty and kindness leave you" (Proverbs 3:3). Don't be despondent; it gives the message of being neutral and not caring. When you're in one of those tough moments that takes every bit of your energy to not turn your back and walk away—*don't*. You are more than that, you are better than that.

You may need to ask for a time out, because you don't trust your ability to be present, loving, and attentive to understand the need at hand. Make that clear, as walking away with no explanation can look and feel more like stonewalling to your partner. But pausing and noticing what you are going through is healthy. We all say and do things in the heat of the moment. You can't take that back; it's better to take a step back and remember who you're talking to. You make better logical sense with a cohesive brain and all parts are working and talking to each other. You can always come back to this issue when things have calmed down, but please be the one to bring it up again if you are the one asking for the time out. Your words are especially powerful at a time like this, be reliable and consistent.

Prayer is a great way to reach out and seek counsel and wisdom from God and others when we feel misunderstood. "I lift up my eyes to the mountains—where does my help come from? My help comes from the LORD, the Maker of heaven and earth. He will not let your foot slip; He who watches over you will not slumber . . . The LORD watches over you--the LORD is your shade at your right hand" (Psalm 121:1-5 NIV). Don't miss an opportunity to hear from Him and others; He may be trying to reach you and show you something very real and powerful that needs your attention.

It takes time and practice to be attentive and to know and understand how you overreact or under-react to conflict. Ask to slow things down if you're struggling to understand. Your relationship is way too important to pretend otherwise. Are you engaging in any of the losing strategies or getting caught in DANGLER? It's worth the time, energy, and patience to pay attention to yourself. Ask an accountability person how they experience you. And if there is anything they see about you that could be harmful to others or yourself. Radical love in a relationship puts aside its own needs, is willing to suspend wants and differences for the sake of another, is courageous and bold to embrace the truth, and puts its ego aside for the sake of love.

CHAPTER 9: RADICAL LOVE AND TRANSFORMATION

May the past be getting further and further behind you as you embrace your new narrative in your recovery and healing process. The word radical has its origins in the word *root*. "Let your roots grow down into Him, and let your lives be built on Him. Then your faith will grow strong in the truth you were taught" (Colossians 2:7). You want to be rooted in the rich fertile soil of God's grace where roots grow deep in the ground and don't get choked by the thorns and thistle of evil.

If your intention is to love unconditionally without any expectations, then you will be strong in the face of adversity. Remember to embrace the pain of recovery and ask God to examine your heart: "Search me, God, and know my heart; test me and know my anxious thoughts. See if there is any offensive way in me, and lead me in the way everlasting" (Psalm 139:23-24). If you have been falsely charged with something you haven't done, remember how much you have been forgiven and the need to forgive others.

I have mentioned that the brotherhood is necessary for growth and accountability; it gives you a safe place to share your issues and hurts. However, it can also be a place where brothers bond over a *shared offense*. If you have not gone before the Lord and examined your heart of any confessions or forgiveness that needs to be addressed in you, you are holding bitterness and wanting company; misery wanting company. This is not the way to use a group. Turning this around and helping your partner heal as you take on ownership while being honest with the brotherhood might look more like: *"I got caught in a lie and denied it to my partner. I admitted the truth after I asked for a respectful time-out to process my shame and forgive myself. I got back to her within the hour to make amends and to admit I was wrong, and to attend extra meetings since I'm clearly in middle circle behavior and manipulating the truth as well as gaslighting her."* Admitting your wrongdoing to the brotherhood, taking ownership, and not dragging them through the fire with you is part of the transformation of the heart. This is taking in a radical change, different from what the norm would want to do. It is humbling and gives the brothers hope. There is no perfect way to reconcile, but speaking the truth in love, is how you will embrace the process of healing and what it takes to recover.

Radical Love for Your Partner

Most partners who have been victims of abuse know the term DARVO. It stands for Deny, Attack, Reverse Victim, and Offender.[81] DARVO describes a common tactic that abusers use to deflect responsibility for their actions. Don't minimize your partner's intelligence; they are working so hard to understand the language and behaviors of sexual integrity issues. Your partner experiences you as the offender in the assault of an intimacy disorder. If you deny, rationalize, pretend to be the victim, or attack her, she will either shut down and feel powerless or get angry and be hyper-vigilant. You may have gotten good at denying and convincing her that she is to blame for her anger, but she may be stuck in high emotions. Being stuck on high can result in anything from rage to risky behaviors that are totally out of her character. It can leave her feeling out of control.

If you are telling yourself that you are now the victim as she stands before you, and potentially screaming in what feels like a threatened state, we now have a complete "reverse victim." According to Dr. Avigail Lev, reversing from the position of the perpetrator to the victim is not going to go well, and it's all part of the crazy-making shifts that can happen in a split second, and particularly when we traumatize each other.[82] Your partner wants nothing to do with DARVO. If you're working your program, attending meetings, seeking accountability, going to counseling, and using your tools, you're doing some good, hard work. If you are angry or flooded, take a deep breath, and work through the S.O.S. (Stop, Orient, Scale) acronym. Have compassion with yourself and your partner. A compassionate response is a gentle notice and will slow you down and give you a better chance of being cohesive and intact.

When you start to sway in the direction of DARVO, run the other way and get back on the right track. With enough practice and attention to the old patterns, you will know when and where to jump off that track. When she is not feeling safe and secure with you, she will let you know, and her defensive mechanism may show up, no different than yours, she is trying to protect herself from any more intrusive thoughts or hurtful behaviors. To avoid falling back into shame and defensiveness, tell yourself, *"It's not me she's afraid of right now; she's scared of the addiction and wants no part of it."* Pull yourself up by the bootstraps and get out of DARVO. The sooner, the better . . . but better late than never.

While you both are in the process of waiting on God and His healing in your lives, get in the habit of going to a place where you can meditate; Jesus went to the garden to pray to the Father. Your prayer might sound like: *"Your will be done, Lord, teach me to love like you, to know your heart and ways, and make me more like you."* Years ago, I heard a friend make an interesting statement that I've held onto as a gentle reminder: *Be Jesus with skin on to others.* Be Jesus to yourself and your partner; it can soften a hardened heart.

Radical love for self and others requires nothing less than surrendering to the one who loves us unconditionally and has given us gifts of love, joy, and peace. He never gives up on us. He cares about our needs and wants. When we ask, He removes the clouds and dark shadows and brings clarity and direction into our lives. He may not answer right away or in the timing we would like, but wait on it, it will come. I prayed over twenty years for God to lift a burden in my heart, and He came through in a beautiful way. It may be the road less traveled, but the things you shall see, hear, taste, and smell along the way will be part of your road map to healing.

We know that not all relationships in the throes of sexual integrity issues will make it through a renewal, but even so, all the work you have put into becoming a new man, going to workshops, meetings, and counseling still matters—all of it matters. Partners are in trauma, and based on the level of infidelity and previous traumas, it can often be complex trauma, which complicates matters even more. They may not have it in them for another round. It would be hard for all involved, including the children, family and friends.

Some stay for various reasons, such as children, finances, and spirituality, while others decide they cannot remain in a relationship with uncertainty. It's not an easy decision for them; their whole world has been turned inside out and upside down. It gets even more complicated when there has been a period of sobriety, and they are trying to build courage and trust to stay, and then there's a relapse and in some cases more and more relapses show up.

Men sometimes tell me they don't want to go through another disclosure, that it will only break her heart again. I don't blame them. I hear their hurt when they say, *"she doesn't have it in her to do this again."* One client, Carl, told me that he keeps looking back, wondering what he missed. He concluded, *"it's always when I don't take the time to be in the word of God on a daily basis."* I am so proud Carl was able to identify a trigger for his addictive behavior, but hear me when I say—*you can be in the Word, go to church, confess your sins, and still find yourself repeating addictive behaviors.* This happens when your roots are not firmly planted, and the thorns and thistles are choking the good roots. Does this mean forget it—it's all for nothing? No, not at all. Don't let Satan feed you any lies. Life can be hard. We are going to suffer and have trials and tribulations. But "don't be surprised at the fiery trials you are going through, as if something strange were happening to you. Instead, be thankful—for these trials make you partners with Christ in His suffering, so that you will have the wonderful joy of sharing His glory when it is revealed to all the world" (1 Peter 4:12). God wants you to draw close to Him in the good and in the bad times. He has great things to teach you, show you, and reveal to you. Joy is waiting to be shared.

Considering a Separation

There is no simple way to recover well without rigorous, radical love and honesty. And as I said, *becoming* takes courageous conversations with yourself and your partner. It takes conforming, introspection, humility, integrative awareness, commitment, compassion, and appreciation. However, not all couples make it to the finish line and one of you might want no part of reconciliation. Working together to create a therapeutic separation agreement before you make the decision to divorce may give you time to pause and think through some options before making any long-term decisions.

It's important that radical love is written all over your separation agreement. It gives you direction and a plan while you both are in the process of deciding on how the future will look. It's also important to work separately to answer the questions thoroughly before reviewing your answers together with your therapist. As written and agreed upon in the separation agreement, you and your partner will get to practice new rules and new ways of relating to one another. You both must be willing to repair, redo, remake, and reform even to consider this contract. You may not know how to calibrate all the adjustments now, but the separation agreement is a start and you can adjust the agreement as necessary and agreed upon throughout the period of separation. It is not a legal document, but rather is a means of setting expectations and new ways of trying on radical love while you work at repairing your relationship. She wants to know that you will go the extra mile to win her heart back to you, and this agreement can be a means of showing up as a man with integrity and truth. (For assistance outlining your own separation agreement, you can access a sample template on my website. This will allow you to edit the template as needed for your own purposes. Please visit the Resources page at the end of this book for more information.)

Before we get into the details of drafting a separation agreement, think about what Carlos wrote as an acronym, PURSUED, as a way of helping him stay focused on his recovery work and intentions.[83] The acronym came to him after his wife said she wanted to be pursued.

Remember Carlos' words as you write out your separation agreement:

- Purposeful: Be purposeful and attentive to her needs.
- Uncomfortable: Be uncomfortable with people, places, and things that distract you from your recovery and help her heal.
- Respect: Be respectful of matters that are important to her.
- Support: Be supportive when her heart is heavy and she needs you to hold her up.
- Understand: Be understanding of her triggers and trauma even if you don't fully get it.
- Emotions: Be in your feelings to understand them.
- Desire: Be passionate about recovery and healing in your marriage.

The most beneficial, therapeutic separation starts with a written agreement that is clearly and thoughtfully put together. It is specifically set up for couples who are focused on their healing and willing to comply and use the tools and recommendations facilitated by their therapist in a clinical setting. During the time of separation, you are to re-evaluate, self-reflect, apply the tools you are learning, recover, heal, practice new ways of engaging and communicating, and learn how to be emotionally accessible to yourself and others.

This is not a good time to make any significant decisions regarding divorce or contacting a lawyer, as it could be seen as a threat to any hope and possibility of repairs for relationship recovery. Any significant purchases, personal expenses, or acting out sexually while working on the separation agreement would not be advised or in your best interest.

Allow individual time to answer each question that's asked and agree on a time to discuss your answers. If you can sit together without the help of your counselor and not allow emotional reactivity to dominate your time, then I would recommend doing this on your own. However, if you cannot come to an agreement or negotiation where there is a win for both parties, and where you both make good efforts to help each other get what the other wants, then you should consider working with your therapist. It is important to agree to take respectful time-outs when one of you is overwhelmed for at least sixty minutes. A time-out may include taking breaks, deep breathing, meditation, walking, or praying. It is a great way to recenter, think clearly and slow yourself down enough to have the ability to ask for what you want. If this process is not going well, even after a few minutes of start-up, it's time to get your counselor involved. (Remember that the time-out model is a good gauge in any future or other discussions you may have. You want to protect yourselves from the *losing strategies*.)

Expectations, fear, challenges, or hesitations can get in the way of completing the separation agreement. This is normal. It could also be a gift in disguise; it's an opportunity for growth, whether you're doing an in-house or out-of-house separation. Keep your word, and do what you know as the right thing to do; seek wisdom and counsel from the wise. Know that God sometimes allows a desperate situation before he delivers. He sees you, and He knows your heart. Whatever your need is, hopefully you can say, *"now I know you are the God that sees me."*

Disappointments are inevitable and temporary. They can be God's way of telling us something more significant is about to happen. We learn in the waiting that he is faithful and does deliver in his timing for His will in each of us. Take the time to figure out what God is trying to teach you in your trials and tribulations. In the New Testament, Paul tells us that he has learned to be content in any circumstances. That takes patience and endurance; we can only do it with God's help.

Leaning into God and what He wants from us in our pain and disappointments is a daily spiritual practice. Don't lose heart; God is faithful and will show up. He wants us to be more and more like Him. He predestined us to be in the image of His son.

Notice what comes up for you in difficult moments, and don't be afraid to sit with it. He sees you and knows what you need. Search your heart. Knowing yourself, understanding what comes up, and communicating your experience to God and others is crucial for your recovery process. You don't have to lose your sobriety over what you think she is expecting of you and what you think is impossible. Don't go into *stinking thinking* and believe you will never be enough. We all have expectations of each other, whether written in a marriage contract or nonverbal. They are formed as children and throughout our life's experiences. Whether you are right or wrong, it never hurts to examine your heart and ask: *"How are my expectations helpful or harmful right now?"* They come out of culture, race, ethnicity, religion, media, and experiences, impacting how we trust, love, rely on, and have compassion for one another.

Some of our expectations are worth abandoning; they have taken up too much residence and become a controlling factor. For example, you may think it's your responsibility to manage the finances for your household because that's the way it was done in your family. It could very well be that your partner states in her separation agreement that she wants to be the one to handle the money. You may not have done so well managing the financial affairs in your active addiction.

> *"Therefore, as God's chosen people, holy and dearly loved, clothe yourselves with compassion, kindness, humility, gentleness, and patience. Bear with each other and forgive one another if any of you has a grievance against someone. Forgive as the Lord forgave you. And over all these virtues put on love, which binds them all together in perfect unity. Let the peace of Christ rule in your hearts, since as members of one body you were called to peace."* Colossians 3:12-15

Some behaviors and expectations must go away for healing to have its way. We must put Christ first to experience victory in the redoing of our lives. This is truly radical love, and we have a perfect example of it. You may experience success without putting Christ first in your life. But, as creatures created by God, we were designed in the image of God to have a relationship with him; we have nothing but His best, working for us and, at best, preparing a place for us while we prepare our hearts for what He has done for us.

QUESTION FOR THE HEART

What holds you back from loving with compassion and kindness toward yourself?

Chapter 10

PEACE AND PROSPERITY

"For I am planting seeds of peace and prosperity among you." Zechariah 8:12

The Bible tells us that "God will generously provide all you need" (2 Corinthians 9:8). I believe that by choosing to leave your old life behind you and press into what lies ahead, based on God's principles and values, you will experience peace and prosperity.

The evil one intends to harm and destroy us, while God's intent is for our good. We are told to be on the alert, to pay attention, and to listen carefully to what He wants us to hear from His word. We are to see into and, "Let them penetrate into your heart, for they bring life to those who find them, and healing to their whole body" (Proverbs 4:21, 22). The Bible also tells us in Proverbs to carry out God's instructions and guard them, because they lead us to wisdom and influence the path of prosperity. "Take hold of my instructions; don't let them go. Guard them, for they are the key to life" (Proverbs 4:12).

The word *idol* is mentioned over two hundred times in the Bible. An idol is anything we put above God, any person or thing that takes precedence in our lives, and all-consuming of precious time that robs us of time with family and friends. Some of the common idols we obsess about include wealth, success, sports, food, exercise, work, lust, identity, looks, phones, and relationships, to name a few. Any of these idols play havoc on our peace and fulfillment in life. Do you serve one or any of these as an idol in your life? What must be cleared and cleaned up in your heart and life to serve God with a pure heart and experience the gift of a "peace that surpasses all understanding"? Take a moment to examine your heart and see if any of these idols get in the way of your peace and prosperity.

Addiction has a propensity to lead with *all or nothing thinking*, going from one extreme to another. It's been said that in recovery, there is often an exchange of one addiction for another. In other words, you may not be searching the web to support your addiction anymore, but in exchange you may obsess about finding fault in others or yourself, the need for instant gratification, perfectionism, food, or smoking. But recovery is more about progress, a continuation of moving beyond what you may not think you are capable of. Think of recovery as a lifestyle; it is your new way of doing life. Your life as you know it now is thought out carefully and planned for success even as we go through the daily grind of life. It is in the process of enduring and going through the difficult trials of *becoming* that you experience the power of change and a transformed heart. In Ezekiel 36:26, God promises: "I will give you a new heart and put a new spirit in you; I will remove from you your heart of stone and give you a heart of flesh" (NIV). Proverbs warns us not to "eat the bitter fruit of living their own way, choking on their own schemes. For simpletons turn away from me—to death. Fools are destroyed by their own complacency. But all who listen to me will live in peace, untroubled by fear of harm" (Proverbs 1:32-33). Don't rush into anything that promises quick deliverance. Be steadfast and remember to "be still and know that I am God" (Psalm 46:10). Seek Him with your heart, soul, and mind, and He will direct your path.

If you're losing your sobriety more than maintaining it, you are not experiencing the peace that is beyond all understanding. Matt walked into my office, reporting that he had lost his sobriety. *"Matt,"* I said, *"What are we doing that isn't working so well?"* Matt couldn't answer that question.[84] Meanwhile, Matt was doing some hard work on his trauma egg, attending meetings, and had an accountability person. However, he lacked the understanding required to recognize middle circle behavior, people, places, events, behaviors, or mood swings that trigger inner circle behaviors. Triggers that lead to inner circle behaviors need to be addressed as idols that consume you with obsessive and compulsive behaviors. Matt doesn't want to live like this; he works way too hard to maintain his sobriety. He is learning to recognize when something is off with him and how it impacts him.

The cycle of addiction has no boundaries and requires you to always be alert and on guard. Think of your middle circle behaviors as rubbish, "counting it all as garbage, so that I could gain Christ" (Philippians 3:8). In moments when you lack understanding and insight into your behaviors and feelings, search for the hidden treasure and promises that God will guide you through. Paul prays that "you will keep on growing in knowledge and understanding. For I want you to understand what really matters, so that you may live pure and blameless lives" (Philippians 1: 9-10). He also says, "I love you and long for you with the tender compassion of Christ" (Philippians 1:8).

God wants us to understand why we do the things we do. It's difficult to dive deep into our stories and hoping to come out on the other side as a self-actualized person. We're making discoveries of what it means to reach our full potential and emotionally developed selves. It takes time, self-reflection, therapy, and money. One of the things that impresses me about the partners I work with is how they are more than willing to help their husbands in the recovery process. It's a huge sacrifice for her when you attend two to three weekly meetings, counseling, etc. The burden of the family and household lies heavily on her, not to mention the financial burden; all the while, she is working on healing herself. The added stress can be a massive distraction for her healing process, but mostly, I find that she wants you to get better and experience peace and healing. You are worth it to her.

Meet the Bravehearts: *Suzanne and Tony*

Below is a testimony from a woman I've worked with who's experienced the complexity of betrayal trauma. As you read her story, you can't help but be impressed with the work she and her husband did as a couple to help her heal. It wasn't perfect, but Tony was willing to do whatever it took to be there for her, and in some of her most traumatic moments, he never left her side. Tony is committed to making a living amends to Suzanne. He has been and still is unwavering and devoted to his recovery work. He has done much of his trauma work and is committed to understanding what triggers and idols that get him into trouble.

Suzanne experienced severe trauma in her childhood, and marrying a man with sexual integrity issues compounded her diagnosis with Complex Post-Traumatic Stress Disorder (CPTSD). She was intuitive and curious when Tony disclosed. She had many questions and Tony answered; however, he didn't disclose the whole truth. Everything about her spirit and soul was damaged with his withholding and lies. He answered any new questions she had, but the full truth still trickled in for many months to come. There were numerous disclosures and more and more questions. She could barely hold it all together. Her most significant and endeared adult relationship with Tony led to abandonment, rejection, and fear of the cycle of addiction repeating itself over and over. Tony was so remorseful and determined to see her through this, and she was resolved to know that he could endure her pain, hold her up, and not walk away in some of her most difficult times.[85]

This couple went through a very difficult time for a long period. They sincerely loved each other and only wanted the best for each other. They both desperately wanted healing and recovery. They worked so hard to get through the repairs and damage of sexual integrity issues. Watching them experience this heartbreaking rupture in their marriage was painful. They did the hard work of delving in with the endless questions Suzanne had and often late into the night. Tony learned what radical truth was about: no more lies and no more acting out. He was willing to do the polygraphs, check-ins whenever he went anywhere, send pictures of his location, not watch TV on his own, and not be left alone with his computer.

Tony had his own childhood wounds to address, yet her trauma overshadowed the level of care she needed for safety and stability. She feared being left alone and worried that he would eventually leave her when she was better. They didn't do this perfectly—who does? They both had moments when they felt the process was overwhelming and wanted to give up. At some point she took some time for herself and went away for a bit to gain some independence and test her ability to do life on her own, in case it got that far. This turned out to be such a brave thing from the condition she started with and going off on her own having to trust herself to not be on watch of his daily activities. Fortunately for their marriage, the heart grew fonder in their absence of one another. It speaks to how hard and how much this couple loves each other.

Being radically honest requires selfless, unconditional, relentless, and untiring persistence. Your partner's trauma and betrayal response are unique to her, and a big part of the work you do is to figure out how she needs your help and how you get the help you need so she can heal. It's a lifelong experience; you're in it for the long haul. As you read Suzanne's testimony below, you will see the beautiful love story they experienced despite all their hardships. Suzanne writes, *"I am free from horrible fear that he may do it again."* It took years of rebuilding trust in herself, managing the ongoing triggers, and trusting that Tony *"will never do it again."*

Suzanne's discovery day came halfway through graduate school. She didn't think she had it in her to finish school; life couldn't have gotten any worse. Suzanne lost her dream of becoming a therapist, her motivation, and her energy.

"Suzanne," I said, *"we're doing this, we're going to get you through this."* She was fragile, scared, and frozen in her trauma. I held her heart and we walked through this journey. Never alone, always putting God in His rightful place, she learned to lean on Him. *"You're not quitting on your dream to be a marriage therapist; you've worked way too hard to let this go,"* I said. And praise God, she now has her license as a marriage counselor. I am so proud of Suzanne and Tony; they never gave up on each other. When she sat for her license examination, he sat outside the test site for four hours so she could focus and not think about what he might be doing or where he might go. He stayed and never left her sight through some of the hardest moments. He proved to be a man of his word.

Later, Suzanne wrote me to explain that her husband's therapy sessions were the catalyst to him being able to fully grasp the impact of his addiction and how it affected every aspect of Suzanne's life. She noted that her husband agreed to another polygraph test, and how crucial it was for their healing that he remain committed to his sexual addiction meetings. Suzanne also noted that some of the things they've agreed to as part of his healing simply haven't happened, for one reason or another. Accountability is important to the healing process—on both sides—and I'll remind her, just like I'd remind you, that in order to maintain integrity and trust in a relationship, holding to the terms of their agreements and vows is nonnegotiable. Suzanne continues to explain the relief she feels considering his healing and how their lives are made more full because he chose to take the step towards recovery and they both are committed to working towards a healthier relationship with themselves and each other.

> "The peace I find today has come from enormous work on our couple-ship and individually. We attend Recovering Couples Anonymous (RCA). We have been in and out of marriage therapy. We also both attend another joint twelve-step program regularly. We participated in a couples group run by Françoise through a church community for a couple of years. We have split and split again (short-term each time). We have gone on retreats, made silent retreats, and sat in pews and on cushions to pray and meditate. We have practiced communication tools, reflective listening, and Fair Communication agreements. We do community giving together. We show up for family and friends."

Suzanne also notes that her husband strives to make amends to her in many ways and that he is willing to do whatever is needed to help her heal. He's cared for her in intimate ways, showering her and getting her ready when grief is too much, and has given her space to feel whatever emotions are necessary in each moment. He has continued to provide answers to her many questions, even staying up through the night to ensure she's heard and seen. He has shown up for family in difficult situations, cooked meals more often, checked in when he was out running errands, and censored his media input. When his lies continued after discovery, he answered Suzanne's intense 150 questions about his behavior. He will grab her hand if there's a triggering person in their path. For the first couple of years, he went everywhere with her because she was terrified that he would return to his old behaviors if left alone. As time passed, he began to stick up for himself during disagreements and started to share his emotions with her—a sign of trust and honestly and growth for both. His boundaries include setting a timer when he's out shopping by himself and owning a flip phone (instead of a smart phone with internet access). These are just a few of the small but meaningful ways he continues to show he cares, he's listening, and he's guarding his mind and heart from his addiction. Suzanne's letter to me continues:

> "As for me and prosperity, I have just begun to spread my wings. I went on a girlfriend weekend out of state. I don't check his

computer history. I don't rage anymore. I meditate and pray more often. I stayed in school through all of this (studying to be a couples infidelity counselor, go figure). I just got fully licensed, so I am starting to feel like my ambitions are returning. I take better care of my health and drink more water and no coffee. I've stopped telling myself that I am ugly, too fat, or not good enough. I can regulate sooner when triggered and not go into the rabbit hole or drag him down. I stopped wearing wigs and fake tattoos to look younger. I just finished amends work on myself. I asked for abstinence and have been slowly working my way back to physical intimacy. I have maintained healthy boundaries with my own body. I am diligently working to trust my husband by taking his word at face value."

Suzanne notes that she's healing herself as well. While she never had skin-to-skin contact, she is in recovery from a pornography addiction and has been sober since discovery. *"I have stopped raging at him. I do not lie to my husband. I am learning to listen to him more. I am allowing myself to fall in love with him again. I am less self-protecting. I don't think about leaving."* She notes that the hard work for her was in staying, in caring for her husband through this, while accepting that they both struggling with sexual integrity issues. She writes: *"It sure is an awful lot of work and purposefulness, but just like the day of discovery—I loved my husband then, and I love him now. And I believe the same is true for him and his love for me."* Suzanne's goal for her life is to remain strong and capable of caring for herself—while knowing that there is no cure for addiction—in case the floors fall out from under them again.

Suzanne's words come from eight long hard years of mostly being all in, and with the hardship in admitting the scary reality that I can't possibly *do* this anymore. The Bible tells us to seek "first his kingdom and his righteousness; and all these things will be given to you as well" (Matthew 6:33 NIV). Tony and Suzanne took the time to reach out to their higher power. They understood early on in recovery that they were not capable of healing themselves and incorporated a daily practice of going before God and the strength to show up even in their moments of helplessness and despair. I call the couples with redemption stories like Tony and Suzanne's *The Bravehearts*. Before redemption comes a story of hardship, wanting to give up, darkness, hopelessness, desperation, demoralization, resignation, and dejection. It's important to share our stories and give back to the community. There is power and courage in the act of being vulnerable in telling your narrative. It gives others hope that there is redemption in doing the work and sticking to it. We will fall and we are nowhere near perfect. We will pick ourselves up, learn the valuable lessons from our mistakes, and prove ourselves to be better people.

In a recent conversation with Suzanne, she was remembering how she asked Tony if he would be there for her in seven years or would she have to be on the floor in a traumatized state for him to stay. She stated that her experience was over the top in a traumatized state. *"I'm not living like that anymore, I'm not afraid anymore. It doesn't mean it's gone away; I'm not obsessing over his behaviors now. I don't want to live in fear and trepidation and be in that phase of my struggle."* Suzanne referred to powerlessness, *"It might be about that, let it go, the power of surrender, I'm a little scared, 99% good and restored to sanity, I am not going back there, I can't live with daily ruminating thoughts, terrified, paralyzed and overly cautious."* In our conversation, Suzanne came to the realization that the love in her marriage to Tony outweighed the hurt and brokenness they had been through, that their marriage was worth fighting for. This is the reason to not give up, but to continue with all your might and all your courage to be the man you know you are.

Meet the Bravehearts: *Lydia and Josiah*

Before Lydia's tears of joy, she experienced fear that came over her every day, not knowing how to move forward with her family, given Josiah's lies and secret infidelities. She thought the best thing to do was leave, until and unless Josiah was ready to face the storm of a marital crisis and be willing to put aside the secretive life that held him in bondage to sin. Her decision to leave and live in a women's shelter with her children was one of the hardest decisions she'd ever make. And yet, it was part of the journey that brought her back to herself and a deeper relationship with God. In God's perfect timing, Lydia's heart was changed: *"I finally saw my sin that I needed to confess and repent from. I am finally free to love him in a new way, just as my Heavenly Father forgave me and loves me."* [86] To get to a place of peace and prosperity, sometimes we must get to the bottom of the barrel, the lowest possible condition we could ever imagine. Lydia's heart hurt deeply, and to protect and shield herself from any further pain, she built walls around her heart. She hardened her heart to not feel the shame she felt for Josiah as he slipped and relapsed repeatedly. But God gave her a new heart, one that could look inside her pain and see the damage that needed healing. She was able to shed the layers of impurities in her own heart that clouded the vision God had for her marriage. "My flesh and my heart may fail, but God is the strength of my heart and my portion forever" (Psalm 73:26 NIV).

Lydia made the decision to leave her husband, Josiah, after eleven years of marriage and ten years of counseling. She could not see any other way out, and nothing seemed to be working. She writes: *"There were many three am wake-ups, and me pleading with the Lord to answer me in my distress. I was scared to make this move; however, I knew the Lord was leading me in this way by giving me multiple confirmations."* Lydia was so hurt by her husband's manipulation, lies, addiction and adultery that she built a wall between them, and when it was time to begin repairing their relationship, she couldn't see the many ways she had closed herself off from the relationship as a defense. She wrote: *"Our sin looked different, but we both needed heart surgery. It took a separation for me to see my true heart condition."*

Lydia and Josiah navigated a legal separation, where Josiah remained available to her and their kids. He was repentant and tender towards her and worked hard to continue to provide for his family. With lots of therapy and changed behaviors, Lydia decided to try on more time to save their marriage, and she outlined marching orders for the house and strict physical boundaries for the two of them. She still found it hard to trust, and when something would trigger her, she'd say, *"See, I knew he would never change. I am a fool to think that he could."* One day her husband told her: *"I feel like I owe you a billion dollars that I can never repay."* And it was then, her walls of defense came crumbling down. Something in her husband's words that cut into her heart, and she realized she had to change the way she was treating him if their relationship was going to survive. She let the feelings of resentment, bitterness, and anger fade away and she decided to start over. The Lord's kindness released her from the bondage, and she was finally free to love her husband in a new way, just as the Heavenly Father loves her.

The separation was necessary because it provided space for Lydia and Josiah to individually seek God's authority and guidance, breaking the strongholds of the darkness. Lydia notes in her writing, that the verse that gave her strength to press forward during this time was Ephesians 6:12 (NIV): *"For our struggle is not against flesh and blood, but against the rulers, against the authorities, against the powers of this dark world and against the spiritual forces of evil in the heavenly realms."*

Reflecting on a recent family vacation, Josiah writes: *"You know those picture-perfect family photos we share on social media? They're like snapshots frozen in time, capturing smiles and laughter, but they don't tell the whole story. They don't reveal the battles fought, the tears shed, or the mountains climbed behind the scenes."* Their story, like many of the Bravehearts, is one of loss, pain, trauma. Praise God that with much work and effort into their marriage and their relationships with God, they are renewed, and they have a redemption story.

As Josiah and Lydia were separated and considering divorce, they realized they were missing out on the richness of marriage, each making selfish decisions for themselves instead of communicating their needs and wants and hopes for their marriage and lives to each other. *"Work and 'busyness' became our refuge; we became masters at creating distractions around the glaring absence of true connection while creating the facade that we were thriving,"* Josiah explains. Their children witnessed the fallout, the disrespect, and they feared this would be the example of marriage their children would grow up to follow.

Josiah writes: "The enemy knew that if we had a thriving marriage, it would shine a light on the faithfulness of our God, Elohim, who keeps His promises." Prayer became a lifeline, "repentance & forgiveness became a balm for their wounded hearts," and they were able to confront their destructive patterns together, allowing God's light and grace to shine through. This commitment to change and humility allowed Lydia and Josiah to untangle misunderstanding, anger, and resentment, and gave them room for authentic connections, paving the way for healing, reunion, and reconciliation.

Josiah and Lydia's marriage has become stronger than it was before as they've relied on honest communication, faithful prayer, and biblical truths to lead the way. Relearning to communicate, offering forgiveness and repairing their friendship were just some of the challenges they faced as they navigated rebuilding their connection to one another. Their connection is deeper and full of grace and understanding, and there's now a freedom to be authentic with one another—mess and all. As parents, watching their children change and grow through all this is special too—there's room for their children to be themselves, unwavering security, stability, and trust, and an example of marriage that can be a real-life testament to overcoming challenges together. Josiah writes:

> *"Our journey not only reshaped our relationship with each other but also deepened our children's faith in God. Through our mess, they saw His faithfulness in action, His grace pouring out to heal and restore what was broken. Our family is becoming a living testament to the power of God's love, strengthening their trust in Him and grounding their faith in something tangible and real."*

God placed a calling on Josiah and Lydia's hearts to step into a ministry where their story of Grace and Hope can be shared in the darkness of the world. Josiah says, *"We feel a divine urgency to reach out to those who may be navigating similar storms, to extend a hand of compassion and understanding, to offer guidance and support through the trials of marriage and family life."* Josiah's encouragement to anyone who finds themselves in a similar darkness is to seek help from Christ, cling to Him in prayer, connect with trusted friends who will sit with you in your mess, and then to be patient for the power of God's grace to renew your marriage and your family.

The love this couple has been able to rekindle is now stronger than ever. Josiah has become Lydia's anchor, with the courage of a warrior. He stayed in the battle and fought the good fight. After years of dedication to the hard work it takes to be sober, safe, healthy, and honest, they are reaping the benefits of a loving and trusting relationship, and in even bigger and greater ways they ever imagined.

Celebrating birthdays and big events together are now a treasured moment in their lives—something to look forward to after all they've overcome. Lydia declares her love for Josiah after his recent birthday: *"I feel the tides are turning . . . from years of me being a 'fire hose' to your flames to now a burning in my heart for more and you keeping me grounded. Excited for the adventure that waits for us as a Son and Daughter of the Most High King!"*

These last few stories you've read are the reason I write this letter to you and the reason I do the work I do. Each story you have read tells you of individuals and couples that are *Bravehearts*. They have taken their healing and recovery to a deep level, learning profound truths that have changed them to the core of their beliefs. They have learned what truly matters in this life.

I have been praying for you, the readers of this letter, even though I will most likely never meet you. I know God knows who you are, and I trust that He will make the power of His grace and love known to you.

God's Constant Provision Through Change

We're in a continuous flux; life, circumstances, and people all change. I appreciate how God shows up when things feel chaotic and entirely out of our control. There are plenty of times I may not have understood a situation completely, and sometime later I experience, feel, and understand it differently.

When my husband and I moved to Chicago, I was four months pregnant with our first child, and we were leaving our families on the east coast to study the Bible. Our families weren't exactly jumping up and down for our new adventure. We planned to stay in the area for a couple of years and move back. We unexpectedly lived in Illinois for the next forty-five years. Early on, I wanted nothing more than to move back home. I wanted our children to grow up with their cousins, aunts, uncles, and grandparents. I will never forget the birthday party we planned in our little apartment when our firstborn was turning one year old. We were all excited, anticipating our new friends to show up and celebrate, but no one came. I was crushed; that wasn't how it was supposed to be. Over time, I accepted God's will for our family and trusted that He knew where we needed to be while we learned what it meant to surrender to His ways and understand that He is not out to make our lives miserable but to give us His best, as only He knows what is best for us.

I am grateful that God's children are asked to pray for one another. Paul says in Colossians 1:9-10, "We ask God to give you complete knowledge of his will and to give you spiritual wisdom and understanding. Then the way you live will always honor and please the Lord and your lives will produce every kind of good fruit." Since my husband and I are now semi-retired, one of the best things in our marriage, as I mentioned earlier, is taking the time each morning to pray together for our family and friends. Not all our prayers are answered as we would like; and unanswered ones are still being prayed for. I leave that to God, as only He knows the situation best.

I cannot say it more explicitly than Proverbs 2, which tells us:

> *"My child, listen to what I say and treasure my commands. Tune your ears to wisdom, and concentrate on understanding. Cry out for insight, and ask for understanding. Search for them as you would for silver; seek them like hidden treasures. Then you will understand what it means to fear the LORD, and you will gain knowledge of God. For the Lord grants wisdom! From his mouth comes knowledge and understanding. He grants a treasure of common sense to the honest. He is a shield to those who walk with integrity. He guards the path of the just and protects those who are faithful to Him. Then you will understand what is right, just, and fair, and you will find the right way to go. For wisdom will enter your heart, and knowledge will fill you with joy. Wise choices will watch over you. Understanding will keep you safe.*
>
> *Wisdom will save you from evil people, from those whose speech is corrupt. These people turn from the right ways to walk down dark and evil paths. They rejoice in doing wrong, and they enjoy evil as it turns things upside down. What they do is crooked, and their ways are wrong.*
>
> *Wisdom will save you from the immoral women, from the flattery of the adulterous woman. She has abandoned her husband and ignores the covenant she made before God. Entering her house leads to death; it is the road to hell. The man who visits her is doomed. He will never reach the paths of life. Follow the steps of good men instead and stay on the path of the righteous. For only the upright will live in the land, and those who have integrity will remain in it. But the wicked will be removed from the land, and the treacherous will be destroyed."*

He instructs us for our good; he desires that we live in peace and harmony, saving us from evil and corruption that can influence our lives when we acknowledge and take to heart his word. "The Lord is close to all who call on Him, yes, to all who call on Him in truth" (Psalm 145:18).

Maintaining a Healthy Sexuality

I could not get to the end of this book without talking about healthy sexuality. Being at peace with our sexuality comes from the creator who designed our sexuality and sexual experience. In God's eyes, sex is beautiful and shameless. When negative sexual experiences limit our ability to enjoy what God has put together for our enjoyment and procreation, a part of us suffers. When the beauty of a committed love is broken, and boundaries are no longer protected, violations offend the body, mind and spirit. God intended the gift of sex as a way of celebrating our love to one another, and not as a means of abuse. Any other way causes a rupture. For some, the rupture is unrepairable; for the couples that stay together and are willing to work through the pain and endure the time it takes to mend, it is only God who can restore the relationship for husband and wife to enjoy the pleasures of having sex with one another. To rebuild this area of your relationship, you will need to address this next assignment with a gentle spirit, patience, and no judgments. Remember, we're looking for peace and prosperity in all areas of our lives.

Sexual intercourse was designed by God with boundaries within the confines of a marriage. It is meant to celebrate our love by pleasuring one another and producing children. In the Bible, the book Song of Songs is a beautiful love story describing the importance of a sexual relationship. It uses a wealth of figurative language with words full of passion and feelings. It speaks of the relationship starting with courtship and then marriage, conflict resolution, and how the couple passionately renewed their love and commitment during the good and bad times. We have to get to know each other and we do this by asking simple questions about favorite colors or inquiring about an impactful and defining experience. This foundation lays the groundwork for sexual intimacy later.

True intimacy starts with being fully known, and sexual intimacy is the culmination of intimacy. Jason Martinkus writes about ten areas of intimacy in his book *Worthy of Her Trust*. The ten areas of intimacy build upon one another, and we must focus on each area of intimacy to have the ability to fully enjoy the gift of making love with our spouses the way God intended it to be.[87] Many of us have started our relationships by having sex from the start rather than following the model of the ten areas of intimacy, which start with being fully known and then go on to cover areas such as emotional, recreational, and intellectual intimacy and our relationship with God. (For further information on Martinkus' *Ten Areas of Intimacy*, please refer to the Resources page.)

Once you have a better understanding of each area of intimacy, you can identify where you are now and where you'd like to be in six months. What needs to happen to get there, and what are you willing to do to get there? Examine your heart and come up with a plan so that you can move forward toward all areas of intimacy. Remember that true intimacy is not just about the act of sex itself; it's about being known to yourself and others.

I remember throwing my lingerie out after discovering my husband's addiction. I felt used, compared to the images he had looked at. I certainly felt like I was not enough or attractive, which led to a decline in wanting to be intimate. I felt ashamed and undesirable. Most couples I've worked with have put sexual intimacy on the back burner for months and sometimes years. I understand the time it takes to trust and want to be close again. It's important to know how to communicate what you need during intimacy, how to touch, lights on or off, slowing down for a bit, how much or how little foreplay, and trusting your ability to ask for what you want.

I love what Solomon says to his beloved in the book of Song of Solomon: "Kiss me and kiss me again," and she responds with great admiration and love, "You are so handsome, my love, pleasing beyond words!" (Song of Solomon 1:2,16) "How beautiful you are, my darling, how beautiful!" (Song of Solomon 1:15 NIV) God truly desires a special kind of love for couples to enjoy one another. After all, He made us as sexual beings and to be expressed in our rightful relationship in marriage.

So how does a couple get back to true intimacy after a sexual integrity issue? It takes fully knowing yourself and being known to one another. Communicating daily about where we are and how we are progressing in all ten areas of intimacy. I also like using FANOS as a daily check in; FANOS stands for Feeling, Admiration, Need, Ownership, Sobriety/Spirituality.[88]

It directs a conversation to the present needs of an individual and the relationship. The beginning of intimacy is being fully known and knowing your partner. FANOS is a tool in getting to be known and understand each other. Be the one to initiate this tool each day to be known. Starting with a feeling like *"I'm feeling hopeful"* is all good, but not quite enough. Explain *why* you're hopeful. Go deeper; be clear, concise, and concrete.

I worked with a couple that had a one-year plan for an out-of-house separation; however, as it drew closer to a year, we made plans for weekend visits and longer stays over time. They decided whether they were ready for sexual intimacy and sleeping in the same bed together. They worked on getting to know each other all over again, fully being known, emotionally, recreationally, spiritually, as well as non-sexual touch. I recommend reading Bercaw and Bercaw's book, *From the Living Room to the Bedroom*. One of the things I appreciate about their book is the emphasis on what happens outside the bedroom, which makes a difference in what happens in the bedroom.[89] You may want things to progress quicker, and I think most men would when it comes to sexual intimacy—and that's not entirely a bad thing—however, your partner has a voice in this matter, and it's important to take time.

After working together for over one year and addressing his underlying issues, Don now understands how his anger went under-detected and would come out sideways. He and his wife had a very busy lifestyle, but after weeks and months of not being sexually active, he would act out looking at sexual images and masturbate, losing his sobriety. Over time, Don learned that he needed to share his feelings with his wife. Margo, a brilliant woman who works hard at her job, comes home exhausted, forgetting promises for date night, while Don is anticipating that they would be sexually intimate as discussed for date night. When Don expresses his feelings of disappointment, Margo would typically ask why everything is about sex to him. He goes into shame and his anger shows up.[90] We worked on communicating his feelings in a loving, respectful way about his sexual needs: *"I look forward to being with you on our weekly date night, holding you, and making love together. I miss you, your touch, and our communication, especially if it's been a while since we've connected. I don't want to be angry at you and think the worst of you when you are tired and don't follow through with a promise of being sexually intimate on date night. I understand being tired, but I get mad at myself for not saying anything. I've spent too much time there, avoiding it* like it doesn't matter. I don't want to be that person anymore. Could you give me a heads-up and perhaps another alternative if you're not wanting to be intimate with me?" It took some work, risking vulnerability, doing something different, being true to himself, and having the courage to speak to his wife in this way. Peace comes with a cost. Ephesians 4:26 tells us, "Don't let the sun go down while you are still angry." We need to be intentional in communicating our needs in a loving and respectful way that addresses a win–win outcome. We prosper when we consider the needs and interests of the other. Don was now better equipped to reach deep down inside of himself and understand his thoughts and Margo's needs.

I am genuinely excited about what the Lord has prepared for you. You will be amazed! Wait and look for it! Be patient; great things await you! Never give up on yourself, remember there is one that loves and knows your intentions and heart, and wants His very best for you, you are His son, made in His image and likeness.

> *"When I think of all this, I fall on my knees and pray to the Father, the creator of everything in heaven and on earth. I pray that from His glorious, unlimited resources He will empower you with inner strength through his Spirit. Then Christ will make his home in your hearts as you trust in Him. Your roots will grow down into God's love and keep you strong. And may you have the power to understand, as all God's people should, how wide, how long, how high, and how deep His love is. May you experience the love of Christ, though it is too great to understand fully. Then you will be made complete with the fullness of life and power that comes from God."* Ephesians 3:14-19

QUESTION FOR THE HEART

When and where are you most at peace, and how do you experience it?

Conclusion

My letter to you has come to an end. This is my story and that of many others with years of work and experience with men and women working through sexual integrity issues. It is a culmination of men in a full-blown addiction, men in and out of recovery, men holding strong to their convictions of getting through the other side of this present darkness, partners in trauma, and my work with couples. I have really enjoyed this process of sharing with you, and I truly hope you walk away from this letter with renewed hope in yourself and your future. While I know that there are so few resources that treat the man, woman, and the marriage at once, it's not always in your best interest to have one person treating all three aspects of the relationship. It's much wiser at the onset to have your own individual therapist while your partner is addressing her trauma and seeking security and safety with a trusted therapist of her own. When there are individual therapists involved who have your permission to talk with each other, it is so beneficial because we all need to be on the same page. Couples groups are very beneficial, they remind couples that they are not alone. A great resource that Suzanne mentioned in her story is Recovering Couples Anonymous (RCA). (Please refer to the Resources page for more information.)

My work proves to be so rewarding when I catch a glimpse of a man reaching for his wife's hand and a wife welcoming the advance as she forges ahead and allows him to help her heal. They both work so hard to be seen and heard. My writing to men is by no accident. God has brought some amazing men into my practice, and I am thankful for what I have learned from them. Their determination to not look back and press on has inspired me to move forward in my own work.

I have a husband, a son, sons-in-laws, and four grandsons that I love dearly, and they are all navigating their masculinity and manhood through life in a world that permits and indulges in ways that are destructive and far from God's heart. It breaks my heart how hard it must be for them.

Seduction entices and promises to deliver, but instead, it wraps its sinful tentacles around us and squeezes the life out of us. I know how easy it is to be defeated, especially in a world where standards of acceptance demand perfection. If anything, believe in the power of the Holy Spirit; he can change you, he will hold you in those dark, desperate moments, and you will again "overflow with prosperity, and the Lord will again comfort" (Zechariah 1:17).

I love the book of Job. Chapter 28:28 says, "The fear of the Lord is true wisdom; to forsake evil is real understanding." Isn't that the longing of our hearts—an understanding of our ways, hearts, and each other? After many trials and tribulations and far beyond what we could ever experience, Job says, "My ears had heard of you, but now my eyes have seen you" (Job 42:5 NIV). My hope for you, brothers in Christ, is that you will draw closer to Him. He alone can heal your broken and disappointed heart. We become a new creature in Christ when we accept Him in our hearts. He gives us His Holy Spirit that teaches, guides, and directs the course of our life when we surrender our lives to Him.

My last words to you come from the book of Ephesians, written to Christ's faithful followers. God desires for you not to be in bondage to sin and the past. He wants prosperity and peace for you even more than you want it for yourself. The only way to experience freedom and a meaningful life is to stay connected to Him, daily putting on the armor of God. Paul says in his final words to the Ephesians:

> *"A final word: Be strong in the Lord and in his mighty power. Put on all God's armor so that you will be able to stand firm against all strategies of the devil. For we are not fighting against flesh-and-blood enemies, but against evil rulers and authorities of the unseen world, against mighty powers in this dark world, and against evil spirits in heavenly places. Therefore, put on every piece of God's armor so you will be able to resist the enemy in the time of evil. Stand your ground, putting on the belt of truth and the armor of God's righteousness. For shoes, put on the peace that comes from the Good News so that you will be fully prepared. In addition to all these, hold up the shield of faith to stop the fiery arrows of the devil. Put on salvation as your helmet, and take the sword of the Spirit, which is the word of God."* Ephesians 6:10-17

CONCLUSION

There is no question that if you purchased this book and read it in its entirety, you will know that I write from a place in my heart that truly cares for your salvation and recovery. I count it as a blessing and want you to know that I appreciate your time and your reading my letter to you, a brother in Christ.

Please know that I have been praying for you, your recovery, your heart, your marriage, and for a peace that surpasses all understanding.

Your Sister in Christ,
Françoise

"Hold on the pattern of wholesome teaching you learned from me—a pattern shaped by the faith and love that you have in Christ Jesus. Through the power of the Holy Spirit who lives within us, carefully guard the precious truth that has been entrusted to you"

2 Timothy 1:13-14

Acknowledgments

I am eternally grateful to my God, who holds me in His heart and believes the best in me. Without Him in my life, I would still be searching for the Way, the Truth and meaning in life.

For the last fifty-three years, I've been married to my best friend, Dan. He is my confidant, my cheerleader, lover of my heart and soul, husband and father of our four children and eight grandchildren. I am thankful for his unconditional love and support, believing in me and patiently giving me the time to express my creativity and encouraging me to write. I am forever grateful for his journey in *becoming* the man he is today with a heart for the Lord. We've grown up together and been each other's best friend. He's seen the best and the worst in me, and yet, he continues to be the strength and courage I need to be the help-meet God has called me to be in his life.

Together we have lived through many trials and tribulations, and they have served to draw us closer to one another. I love the man Dan has become, a man after God's heart, and for that I've been able to write this book because of the undertaking in our healing.

For my children, I am blessed beyond measure to have each of them in my life, they are my heart, and my joy. I am so proud of each of them. My grandchildren light up my life. I can barely put into words how much I love them. The best I can do is to bring them before the Lord each day and ask for their safety and protection. They are the fulfillment of their parents, and I am thankful for all the ways they have taught me what it means to love without expectations.

I am grateful for the clients who lovingly supported me and eagerly wanted their stories to be told. They were the brave hearts who believed in helping and encouraging one another through their difficult journeys. I appreciate the courage it takes to share their painful narratives as well as offer hope and healing. I admire their willingness to trust me and the vulnerability it takes to be open and honest.

I am grateful for the family and friends who prayed for me and cared enough to ask how I was doing throughout the process of my writing.

Ariel Curry, my editor, your insight and wisdom have inspired me. Your patience and kindness have taken me further along. I am forever grateful for coming across this vibrant young writer and editor at the Drawing Room. Danielle Raymond, another amazing editor, who patiently came along side and instructed me to stay on a path that would be legible and fundamentally make sense to you the reader.

I am grateful for Market Refined Media, a team of strong and knowledgeable women who saw my manuscript and heard my dream and helped me put it to print with their creative and imaginative ideas. I couldn't have done this by myself. It takes a village, and we're not meant to do life alone.

Recommended Resources

Françoise Mastroianni

newreflectionsclinical.com/resources

- ✏ Covenant Template
- ✏ Separation Agreement Template
- ✏ *Spouses of Sex Addicts: Hope for the Journey Workbook*

Patrick Carnes

patrickcarnes.com

- ✏ Core Dialogue exercise from his *Recovery Start Kit*
- ✏ Personal Crazy Index from *The 90-Day Prep*

Dr. Omar Minwalla

minwallamodel.com

- ✏ Thirteen Dimensions of Trauma

John Gottman

gottman.com

- ✏ The History and Philosophy of Your Feelings

Jason Martinkus

jasonmartinkus.com

- ✏ *Worth of Her Trust: What You Need to Do to Rebuild Sexual Integrity and Win Her Back*
- ✏ The Ten Areas of Intimacy from his book *Worth of Her Trust*

SA Lifeline Foundation

salifeline.org

- ✏ "To My Friends and Family, What I Wish You Knew..." (salifeline.org/2019/11/06/to-my-friends-and-family-what-i-wish-you-knew)

Dr. Peter Levine

traumahealing.org

- ✏ Waking the Tiger

Bill Bercaw and Ginger Bercaw

californiahealingcenter.com

- ✏ From the Living Room to the Bedroom

Organizations and Additional Resources

- Rape, Abuse & Incest National Network (RAINN):
  https://rainn.org

- National Sexual Assault Online Hotline:
  https://hotline.rainn.org/online

- National Sexual Assault Hotline:
  1-800-656-4673

- Recovering Couples Anonymous (RCA):
  https://recovering-couples.org

- Sex Addicts Anonymous (SAA):
  https://saa-recovery.org

- Alcoholics Anonymous (AA):
  https://www.aa.org

- Celebrate Recovery:
  https://celebraterecovery.com

- The Crucible Project:
  https://thecrucibleproject.org

- Man Talks Alliance:
  https://mantalks.com

- Brother's Road:
  https://brothersroad.org

- SAMHSA:
  https://www.samhsa.gov

- SAMHSA National Helpline:
  1-800-662-4357

Introduction

1. Merriam-Webster, s.v. "emotion," Merriam-Webster.com Dictionary, accessed April 22, 2025, https://www.merriam-webster.com.
2. Peter Scazzero, *Emotionally Healthy Spirituality Day by Day: A 40-Day Journey with the Daily Office*, updated ed. (Grand Rapids, MI: Zondervan, 2017), 49.

Chapter 1

3. Curt Thompson, *The Soul of Shame: Retelling the Stories We Believe About Ourselves* (Downers Grove, IL: InterVarsity Press, 2017), 72.
4. Doug Weiss, *Helping Her Heal* (DVD).
5. Patrick Carnes, *Don't Call It Love: Recovery from Sexual Addiction* (New York: Bantam, 1991), 90–110.
6. Margery Williams, *The Velveteen Rabbit* (New York: Doubleday, 1922).
7. Bob, client letter, used with permission.
8. Dan Allender and Tremper Longman, *The Cry of the Soul: How Our Emotions Reveal Our Deepest Questions About God* (Colorado Springs, CO: NavPress, 1994), 24–25.

Chapter 2

9. Stefanie Carnes, Mari A. Lee, and Anthony D. Rodriquez, *Facing Heartbreak* (Carefree, AZ: Gentle Path Press, 2012), 13.
10. Sexaholics Anonymous, "The Twelve Steps," accessed 2024, https://www.sa.org/twelve.
11. Peter Scazzero, *Emotionally Healthy Spirituality* (Grand Rapids, MI: Zondervan, 2014), 173.
12. Daniel Siegel, "12 Revolutionary Strategies to Nurture Your Child's Developing Mind, Survive Everyday Parenting Struggles, and Help Your Family Thrive," DrDanSiegel.com, accessed July 7, 2024, https://drdansiegel.com/whole-brain-child-handouts.

Chapter 3

13. Barbara Steffens and Marsha Means, *Your Sexually Addicted Spouse: How Partners Can Cope and Heal* (Far Hills, NJ: New Horizon Press, 2009), 62.
14. American Psychological Association, "Trauma," accessed May 22, 2024, https://www.apa.org/topics/trauma.
15. Omar Minwalla, "Education in Deceptive Sexuality and Trauma Treatment," Institute for Sexual Health, accessed June 5, 2024, https://minwallamodel.com.
16. Minwalla, "Education in Deceptive Sexuality and Trauma Treatment."
17. Jaime, client letter, used with permission.
18. Nora, client letter, used with permission.
19. Bill, client letter, used with permission.
20. Minwalla, "Education in Deceptive Sexuality and Trauma Treatment."
21. Claire, personal interview, used with permission.
22. Minwalla, "Education in Deceptive Sexuality and Trauma Treatment."
23. Emily, client letter, used with permission.
24. Peter Levine, *Waking the Tiger: Healing Trauma* (Berkeley, CA: North Atlantic Books, 1997), 20.
25. Françoise Mastroianni and Richard Blankenship, *Spouses of Sex Addicts: Hope for the Journey Workbook* (Alpharetta, GA: BookLogix, 2013), 37.
26. Alice, client interview, used with permission.
27. Omar Minwalla, "Thirteen Dimensions of Sex Addiction Induced Trauma," Minwalla Model, accessed June 2024, https://minwallamodel.com.
28. Minwalla, "Thirteen Dimensions of Sex Addiction Induced Trauma."
29. Cristy, client letter, used with permission.
30. Tamara, client letter, used with permission.
31. Lori, client letter, used with permission.
32. Riley, client letter, used with permission.
33. Minwalla, "Education in Deceptive Sexuality and Trauma Treatment."
34. Mark, client letter, used with permission.
35. Young Woman, client letter, used with permission.
36. John Ortberg, *Soul Keeping: Caring for the Most Important Part of You* (Grand Rapids, MI: Zondervan, 2014), 141–47.

Chapter 4

37. John Bradshaw, *Healing the Shame That Binds You* (Deerfield Beach, FL: Health Communications, Inc., 2005), 36.
38. Daniel Siegel, *Aware: The Science and Practice of Presence* (New York: TarcherPerigree, 2018), 47.

39. Thompson, *Soul of Shame*, 108.
40. David Benner, *Sacred Companions: The Gift of Spiritual Friendship and Direction* (Downers Grove, IL: InterVarsity Press, 2002), 47.
41. Joseph, client letter, used with permission.
42. John Gottman, *What Makes Love Last? How to Build Trust and Avoid Betrayal* (New York: Simon & Schuster, 2012).
43. Jack, client letter, used with permission.
44. Albert Ellis, *A Guide to Rational Living* (North Hollywood, CA: Wilshire Book Company, 1975), 35.
45. National Science Foundation, accessed August 2024, https://www.nsf.gov.

Chapter 5

46. Alcoholics Anonymous World Services, *Alcoholics Anonymous Comes of Age: A Brief History* (New York: Alcoholics Anonymous World Services, 1957), 64.
47. Alcoholics Anonymous, "The Twelve Steps," accessed May 22, 2024, www.aa.org/the-twelve-steps.
48. James, client letter, used with permission.
49. Jason Martinkus and Stephen Arterburn, *Worthy of Her Trust* (Colorado Springs, CO: WaterBrook, 2014), 199.
50. Bob, client letter, used with permission.

Chapter 6

51. Eric, client letter, used with permission.
52. Patrick Carnes, *Facing the Shadow: Understanding and Overcoming Sexual Addiction* (Center City, MN: Hazelden, 1997).
53. Scazzero, *Emotionally Healthy Spirituality*.
54. U. Dahlen, D. Colpitts, and C. Green, "The Trauma Egg as an Intervention with the Spouses of Sexually Addicted Men," *Sexual Addiction & Compulsivity* 15, no. 4 (2008): 346–54, https://doi.org/10.1080/10720160802516336.
55. Janice Caudill and Dan Drake, *Full Disclosure: How to Share the Truth After Sexual Betrayal* (Independently published, 2020).
56. Carnes, *The 90-Day Prep*, 109.
57. Scazzero, *Emotionally Healthy Spirituality*, 46.
58. Scazzero, *Emotionally Healthy Spirituality*, 39.
59. Scazzero, *Emotionally Healthy Spirituality*, 40.
60. Nathan, client letter, used with permission.
61. Scazzero, *Emotionally Healthy Spirituality Day by Day*, 61.

62. Mother Teresa, *A Simple Path* (New York: Ballantine, 1995), 7–8.
63. Arnold Cole and Pamela Caudill Ovwigho, "Understanding the Bible Engagement Challenge: Scientific Evidence for the Power of 4," Center of Bible Engagement, 2009.
64. Scazzero, *Emotionally Healthy Spirituality*, 63.
65. Scazzero, *Emotionally Healthy Spirituality*, 149.

Chapter 7

66. Scazzero, *Emotionally Healthy Spirituality*, 33–34.
67. Mastroianni and Blankenship, *Spouses of Sex Addicts*.
68. Dan, author's husband, used with permission.

Chapter 8

69. Mark Lasser, *Healing the Wounds of Sexual Addiction* (Grand Rapids, MI: Zondervan, 2004), 19.
70. Lasser, *Healing the Wounds of Sexual Addiction*, 187.
71. Anonymous, "To My Friends and Family, What I Wish You Knew…" SA Lifeline Foundation, November 6, 2019, accessed May 2024, https://salifeline.org/2019/11/06/to-my-friends-and-family-what-i-wish-you-knew.
72. Carnes, *Recovery Start Kit*.
73. Reed, client letter, used with permission.

Chapter 9

74. Coaching for Christ, "What does Radical Living mean?" accessed June 1, 2024, https://coachingforchrist.org.uk/radical-living.
75. Williams, *The Velveteen Rabbit*.
76. Tony A. Gaskins Jr., *Make It Work: 22 Time Tested, Real-Life Lessons for Sustaining a Healthy, Happy Relationship* (New York: Simon & Schuster, 2019), 79–82.
77. Terry Real, "Five Losing Strategies & Five Winning Strategies," Moonstone Counseling, accessed June 5, 2024, https://www.moonstonecounseling.com/uploads/1/2/0/4/120459773/five-losing-strategies-five-winning-strategies.pdf.
78. Real, "Five Losing Strategies & Five Winning Strategies."
79. Ellen, client letter, used with permission.
80. Terry Real, "Standing Up to One Another with Love," Sounds True Interview, https://resources.soundstrue.com/podcast/terry-real-standing-up-to-one-another-with-love.

81. Jennifer Freyd, "Violations of Power, Adaptive Blindness, and Betrayal Trauma Therapy," *Journal of Feminist Psychology*, 2017.
82. Freyd, "Violations of Power, Adaptive Blindness, and Betrayal Trauma Therapy."
83. Carlos, client letter, used with permission.

Chapter 10

84. Matt, client story, used with permission.
85. Suzanne and Tony, client story, used with permission.
86. Lydia and Josiah, client story, used with permission.
87. Martinkus and Arterburn, *Worthy of Her Trust*.
88. Deborah Laaser, *Shattered Vows* (Grand Rapids, MI: Zondervan, 2008), 184–186.
89. Bill Bercaw and Ginger Bercaw, *From the Living Room to the Bedroom* (California Center for Healing, 2014).

About the Author

Françoise is known among her friends and clients for her compassion, listening skills, directness, fearlessness, wisdom and spiritual support. She spent years volunteering in community-based organizations as a counselor with Care Net Pregnancy Services, and local health department.

With her children launched, Françoise professionalized her skills and added to her life experience a Master of Science in Human Services Counseling from National Louis University. She attained licensure as a licensed Clinical Professional Counselor (LCPC), and has added many other certifications, including working as a sexual addiction specialist, working with partners, somatic work, hypnotherapy, and other specialties to better equip, help, and treat her clients. Françoise has taught college-level courses related to her field and authored *Spouses of Sex Addicts: Hope for the Journey Workbook*.

In 2004 Françoise launched a private practice, New Reflections Clinical Services, specializing in alcohol/substance abuse, sexual addiction, body work and trauma. Individuals and couples have traveled distances to work with Françoise, and she continues to engage with compassion, wisdom and a deep understanding of God's design for human sexuality and marriage. These qualities and experiences have positioned Françoise to write this book with prayers that it will indeed provide hope and healing in some of the most powerful and deepest areas of life.

In her leisure time, Françoise enjoys painting furniture, hiking, cooking, spending time with family and friends, traveling, and reading.

www.ingramcontent.com/pod-product-compliance
Lightning Source LLC
Chambersburg PA
CBHW080919170426
43201CB00016B/2195